D1506371

French Phrase Book

1,500+ Common French Phrases and Vocabulary for Beginners and Travelers

"Best blog dedicated to the French Language and Culture for 2014, 2015, and 2016."

(voted by the Language Portal blab.la and its community)

Also available:

French Short Stories for Beginners

(https://geni.us/fssbvol1)

French Grammar for Beginners

(https://geni.us/frenchgrammar)

For more products by Frédéric BIBARD/Talk in French, visit :

https://www.amazon.com/Frederic-BIBARD (for US)

https://www.amazon.co.uk/Frederic-BIBARD (for UK)

Or go to https://store.talkinfrench.com.

Table of Contents

Introduction

Traveling to France, or any French-speaking country, can be quite daunting. I'm sure you've heard some terrible things about being a tourist in France, like how haughty waiters ignore your orders, or how French people, especially the Parisians, can be just downright rude and unwilling to help tourists. As a French man who spends a lot of time talking to foreigners, I've heard this all before. And though I know how traveling in France can be a bittersweet experience, I believe this is just a general misunderstanding that can be fixed by two things:

1. Better communication
2. Some background on French culture

You would be amazed at how a simple "Bonjour," "merci," or "s'il vous plait" can be a game changer when dealing with sales clerks, waiters, or any French person on the street. Even if you're able to communicate just a tiny bit in French, I guarantee that you will have a totally different experience in my country.

Such is the reason that I created this book: to help address those two things I mentioned above. With this book, I want to make your traveling experience in France as smooth as possible by giving you all the phrases and vocabulary you need to communicate in French in a simple way.

But just to be clear: this book will not teach you French. Instead, it is designed to serve as a great guide to help you find your way through all the possible scenarios as a tourist in France. It will help you know the right words to say from the moment you arrive at the airport to sightseeing, shopping, dining and even during emergencies.

I have also included bonus material to give you some background on French culture, as well as to make dining in France a very pleasant experience.

Here's what you'll find inside:

- 1,500+ French words and expressions with English translations. This includes an easy phonetic pronunciation guide (e.g. bonjour = bon•zhoor).
- Audio to help you practice your listening and pronunciation skills in French.
- A menu reader to help you order the right food. Refer to 600+ food vocabulary and French dishes translated from French to English.
- A pronunciation guide.

Aside from tourists, this book will also benefit those who wish to jumpstart their French language lessons. If you are a beginner level learner, or you have previously studied French and would like to review some basic phrases, this book is also great for you.

I hope you'll enjoy this book.

Merci,

Frédéric BIBARD
Founder, Talk in French

Advice on how to use this book effectively

Take this book with you when you travel to France, and see how your level of confidence will greatly improve.

This book is arranged according to theme in order to make searching easier for you. Whatever scenario you find yourself in, just flip over to that page and take a look at the list of phrases listed. The first column contains the French phrase, the second column is for the English translation of the phrase, and the third column is the easy phonetic pronunciation guide.

This book comes with 89 minutes of French audio to boost your listening and pronunciation skills, as well as several other bonus features. Follow along with the high-quality audio narrated by a native French speaker to help train your ear to the sound of authentic words and phrases as spoken by natives.

On the last page of this book (Page 157), you will find the link for downloading the audio files that accompany this book. Save the files onto any device and listen to it anywhere.

Important! The link to download the Audio Files is available at the end of this book. (Page 157)

Part 1 – Basic lessons

Lesson 1: Mastering Pronunciation

How to pronounce French the right way

There is a charming quality to the spoken French language that most people find utterly delightful. The way in which the words seem to melt together to form pleasant sounds and flowing melodic tones can be both enchanting and intimidating at the same time. It is enchanting enough for those who are not French to strive to replicate its romantic-sounding inflections, but very intimidating when you listen to French people actually speak.

No need to get intimidated for long, though. By choosing this guide, you are already on the right track for learning how to speak French because this section is solely focused on proper French pronunciation. Whether you are beginning to learn the language or you simply need to brush up on your intonation, this is the perfect tool for you!

The study method and guide presented below are formulated for English speakers and will help you to grasp the pronunciation rules better. It can be tricky for newbie learners, but with regular practice in speaking and reading, you should be able to do quite well soon enough. Remember, you do not need to memorize these rules; by referring to this guide consistently, you will improve in no time. So study it as often as you'd like! It will be ingrained in your mind before you know it.

Here is a tip from a native French speaker (aka me):

Don't be too hard on yourself when you can't fully grasp the pronunciation rules after a few hours of practice. It takes time to learn how to pronounce French words properly – months, in fact. Besides, it's extremely rare to see a foreigner with 100% correct pronunciation. But does it really matter? France is a hugely multicultural country and the French people are quite familiar (and accepting!) of a wide range of accents. So don't beat yourself up, and just keep practising until you start to pull off French quite nicely.

So are you ready? Here we go!

Lesson 2: The stress (and why you shouldn't stress out about it)

When compared to the English language, French has a more distinct sound and a flat intonation. The stress is mostly even except for the last syllable, which is given a bit more emphasis. Check out the following example using the word 'important'.

Notice the difference in stress between the English and French pronunciations:

Listen to Track 1

<u>English</u>: im-**_POR_**-tant

<u>French</u>: _ang-**por-tah**ng_

See the difference?

Lesson 3: How to pronounce French vowels

For the newbie French learner, understanding the difference between **a, à,** and **â,** as well as **e, é, è,** and **ê,** can be head-swimmingly frustrating. However, the truth is it's not actually that complicated. Below is a nifty guide to help you easily distinguish between the pronunciation of each of the letters and their mind-boggling accents, or diacritical marks (those little *thingies* on top of the letters):

Listen to Track 2

Vowels	Pronunciation Guide	Example	What the example means
a	is pronounced like 'ah' in English	la	(the)
à	is also pronounced like 'ah	là	(there)
â	is pronounced like 'ah' but longer	àne	(donkey)
e	When placed in the middle of a syllable, it is pronounced like ai in 'fair'	mer	(sea)
e	When placed at the end of a syllable, it is pronounced like er in 'her'	le	(the)
e	is silent at the end of a word	tasse	(cup)
é	is pronounced like 'ay'	été	(summer)

è	is pronounced like ai in 'fair'	père	(father)
ê	is also pronounced like ai in 'fair'	tête	(head)
i, y	are pronounced like ee in 'meet'	ski	(skiing)
o	is pronounced like o in 'not'	poste	(post office)
ô	is pronounced like 'oh'	hôtel	(hotel)
u	this sound does not exist in English; say 'oo' with rounded lips	vu	(seen)
oi	is pronounced like 'wah'	roi	(king)
ou	is pronounced like 'oo'	roue	(wheel)

Easy enough? Here is a quick recap on the vowel pronunciations:

- **a** and **à** are both pronounced 'ah' in English.
- **â** is also pronounced 'ah', except the sound is held longer.
- **e, è,** and **ê** placed in the middle of a syllable, are pronounced 'ai' as in *fair*.
- The rule for pronouncing **e:** in the middle of a syllable, it is pronounced 'ai' as in *fair*; at the end of a syllable, it is pronounced 'er' as in *her*; at the end of a word, it is silent (e.g. *tasse*).

Now we will move on to the consonants.

Lesson 4: All about consonants

Consonants in French are basically pronounced the same as they are in English. Here is a quick guide to help you remember them:

Listen to Track 3

Conso-nants	Pronunciation Guide	Example	What the example means
c	before e or i sound like s	ceci	(this)
c	elsewhere it sounds like k	car	(coach)
ç	sound like s	ça	(that)
ch	sound like 'sh'	château	(castle)
g	before e or i sounds like s in 'measure'	général	(general)
g	elsewhere sounds like g in 'go'	gare	(station)
h	is silent	hôtel	(hotel)
j	sounds like s in 'measure'	je	(l)
qu, q	sounds like k	qui	(who)
r	is pronounced at the back of the throat; it is quite similar to the sound we make when are gargling	rire	(to laugh)
s	at the beginning of a word sounds like s	salle	(room)
s	between two vowels, it sounds like z	rose	(rose)

Note: Except for the letters **c, f, l,** and **r**, consonants are not usually pronounced when they appear as the last letter of a word. For example, the **t** at the end of *passepor(t)* and the **s** at the end of *Pari(s)* are silent.

However, **c, f, l** and **r** are pronounced, such as in the words *hôtel* and *professeur*.

To help you remember that these four consonants are exceptions, you can use this mnemonic device: **C**lear **F**rench **L**anguage **R**ecall or CFLR.

(See, told you this is easy!)

Lesson 5: What are French nasal sounds?

Most non-French speakers will usually describe the French language as having a "nasal" sound to it. These nasal sounds are quite distinctive of the French language and are characterized by the following:

1. They are produced by the blocking of air from leaving the mouth, causing it to be released through the nose.

2. These sounds are 'voiced,' which means the vocal cords vibrate to create the sound.

Sounds difficult? Not actually. In fact, the English language has three nasal sounds too, namely the 'm' sound, the 'n' sound, and the 'ng' sound. We are using these to speak flawlessly (or not!) every day.

Try saying the words *sing, sang, song* and *sung* and you will notice the following: the letter **g** is given very little value in the standard pronunciation, and as you pronounce the words, air is blocked when the back of your tongue presses against the soft palate.

French has four nasal sounds that are more similar to their English counterparts than we realize. They are as follows:

Listen to Track 4

Nasal sound	Pronunciation	Example	What the example Means
om, on	pronounce like ong in 'song'	nom non	(name) (no)
um*, un	pronounce like ung in 'sung'	un brun	(one) (brown)
am, an em, en	pronounce like 'ahng'	champ an temps en	(field) (year) (time) (in)
im*, in, aim, ain, ein	pronounce like ang in 'sang'	simple vin faim bain plein	(easy) (wine) (hunger) (bath) (full)
ien	pronounce like 'ee-ang'	bien	(well)

We mentioned that there are four nasal French sounds, so you may be wondering why there are five listed. This is because some French speakers do not make a distinction between **um*** and **im,*** pronouncing both as 'ang' like we do in *sang*.

Listen to Track 5

Sylla-ble	Pronunciation	Example	What the Example Means
er	at the end of a word of two syllables or more sounds like 'ay'	parler	(to speak)
ez	at the end of a word sounds like 'ay'	nez	(nose)
ail	at the end of a word sounds like 'ah'ee'	travail	(work)
eil, eille	sounds like 'a'ee'	soleil bouteille	(sun) (bouteille)
ill	usually sounds like 'ee'y'	billet	(ticket)
gn	sounds like ni in 'onion'	signal	(signal)

Lesson 6: All the French-Y variations

Now read carefully because this is where non-French speakers often get into trouble. Listed below are some pronunciations for syllables that, when spoken, differ quite a bit from how they are pronounced in English:

Er (when at the end of a word with two or more syllables) and **ez** are both pronounced like 'ay'. As an exception to the **c, f, l, r** consonants pronunciation rule presented earlier, **l,** when used in the syllables **ail** and **eil**, is generally silent. Surely you are quite familiar with the '**gn**' sound already (especially if you are the lasa**gn**a-eating type!).

Lesson 7: Those flowing, connected sounds and how it is done

We are all quite aware that the French language has a flowing and uninterrupted quality to its sound, or to put it jokingly, it sounds like one is speaking in cursive. This lends the language a lot of charm and a very noticeable melodic sound that foreigners simply love.

To achieve this delightfully melodious sound in your speech, here is a simple rule for you to remember:

If a word that begins with a vowel or a silent **h** follows a word that ends in a consonant, the consonant is linked to the beginning of the second word.

Simply stated, *if*:

1st word — ends in a consonant, *and*

2nd word — begins with a vowel or silent H

Result: the consonant at the end of the first word is automatically linked to the beginning vowel of the second word.

To illustrate this concept, here are a few examples:

Listen to Track 6

1. *nou**s a**vons* – the first word (*nous*) ends with a consonant, while the second word (*avons*) begins with a vowel.

Pronunciation: noo **zah**-vong (meaning 'we have'*)*

2. un peti**t e**nfant – the first word (*petit*) ends with a consonant, while the second word (*enfant*) begins with a vowel.

Pronunciation: ung p'tee **tahng**-fahng (meaning 'a small child')

Here are a few guidelines to remember when using other letter combinations:

Listen to Track 7

Letters	Sound	Example	Pronun- ciation	What the example means
s, x	sounds like z	deux ans	der zahng	two years
d	sounds like t	un grand arbre	ung grahng tahbr	a tall tree
f	sounds like v	neuf heures	ner verr	nine hours

Lesson 8: Accent marks (and the difference they make)

Just like several other languages, the French language makes use of accent marks. Accents are a type of diacritic mark, which is basically a glyph, or a small sign attached to a letter. These are commonly used in Latin-derived alphabets as well as non-Latin ones like Chinese, Arabic, Greek, Hebrew, and Korean.

French makes use of three main accents:

Listen to Track 8

- The acute accent (**é**) or *l'accent aigu,* which can be found with the letter **e**
- The grave accent (**è**) or *l'accent grave,* which can be found with the letters **a, e,** and **u**
- The circumflex (**ê**) or *l'accent circonflexe* which can be found with any vowel

In addition, there is the cedilla (**ç**) or *la cedilla,* which can be found only underneath the letter **c,** and the diaeresis (**ë**) or *le tréma,* which is often used to indicate that the second vowel is to be pronounced separately from the first (e.g. *naïf,* which means 'naive,' and *Noël,* which means 'Christmas').

So, what are accent marks for? you might ask. Here are their uses:

First, they are used to change how a letter sounds. Let's take for example the letter **e**. The unaccented **e** sounds like 'er' in *her.* The **é** acute sounds like 'ay' in *say.* The **è** grave sounds like 'ai' in *fair.*

For the cedilla, remember the rule discussed earlier wherein **c** is only pronounced as a soft **s** when placed before an **e** or **i**? The cedilla totally changes that. Take for example the word *garçon* (which means 'boy'). It precedes an **o**, which means it should be pronounced as a hard **c** as in *car*, but the cedilla softens the letter to make it sound like an **s** as in *sit*.

Second, accent marks are used to differentiate between similarly spelled words that have different meanings.

Examples:

Listen to Track 9

- **la** (the) versus **là** (there)
- **ou** (or) versus **où** (where)
- **sur** (on) versus **sûr** (sure)

There is something very interesting about the accents, however. In modern usage, French accents usually do not appear in capital letters because it is deemed unnecessary. The Académie Française, however, maintains that accents should be used at all times in order to avoid confusion.

Lesson 9: French and English similarities

Contrary to popular belief, there is not a significant difference between English and French pronunciation. In fact, most syllables are pronounced as though they are part of an English word and are each given equal stress.

However, take note of the following rule while reading the examples shown in this guide:

Listen to Track 10

- ***ng* (italics)** – must never be pronounced; these letters merely indicate that the preceding vowel has a nasal sound.
- **zh** – sounds like s in 'measure'.
- **ü** – no equivalent in English; round your lips and say 'ee'.
- **o** – sounds like o in 'not'.
- **oh** – sounds like o in 'note'.

Lesson 10: The French alphabet

The French Alphabet also contains 26 letters of the ISO basic Latin-script alphabet (or, simply, the alphabet as we know it). It is similar to the English alphabet except for **K** and **W,** which are not always used. The names of the letters are also a bit different. So, just in case you are planning to visit France soon, you might want to practice spelling your name out phonetically if the French-speaking receptionist (or other people essential to your travel) require it. Spelling it out in French phonetically would make a lot more sense to them than using the English alphabet.

Here is an example:

If your name is JANEY, it is spelled out as *'zheel – ah – en – er – ee-grek'*.

Here is the rest of the French alphabet as well as the letters' pronunciations:

Listen to Track 11

A (ah)	**B (bay)**	**C (say)**	**D (day)**	**E (er)**
F (ef)	**G** (zhay)	**H** (ahsh)	**I** (ee)	**J** (zheel)
K (kah)	**L** (el)	**M** (em)	**N** (en)	**O** (oh)
P (pay)	**Q** (kü)	**R** (aair)	**S** (ess)	**T** (tay)
U (ü)	**V** (vay)	**W** (dooblvay)	**X** (eeks)	**Y** (ee-grek)
Z (zed)				

Try to practice saying these pronunciations as often as you can, as this will help you advance in your learning. Remember, just like any other skill, all it takes is determination and consistency for you to develop the habit. Exposing yourself to the French language in movies, videos, and even audio books can help you become more familiar with the words and sounds, making it easier to learn them.

Part 2 – French phrases

Chapter 1: Essentials / L'essentiel

Chapter 1.1: The French basics / Les bases du français

This chapter will be the most useful when you need help getting out of a difficult situation.

__Listen to Track 12__

French	English	Pronunciation
Bonjour. / Salut. (informal)	Hello. / Hi.	*boñ-zhoor. / sa-lew.*
Au revoir. / Salut.	Goodbye. / Bye.	*oh ruh-vwar. / sa-lew.*
Pardon, monsieur/ madame !	Excuse me! (to catch attention)	*par-doñ, muh-syuh/ma-dam !*
Pardon !	Sorry!	*par-doñ !*
Je suis désolé(e).	I'm sorry.	*zhuh swee day-zo-lay.*
Merci (beaucoup).	Thanks (very much).	*mehr-see {boh-koo).*
S'il vous plaît.	Please.	*seel voo pleh.*
Parlez-vous anglais ?	Do you speak English?	*par-lay-voo ahn-gleh ?*
Y a-t-il quelqu'un ici qui parle anglais ?	Does anyone here speak English?	*Ya a-tteel kel-kuhn eesee kee par long-gley ?*
Je ne parle que l'anglais.	I speak only English.	*zhuh nuh parl kuh long-gley.*
Je parle un peu français.	I speak a little French.	*Zhuh parl uhn puh frahn-seh.*

Listen to Track 13

Veuillez parler plus lentement.	Please speak more slowly.	*vuh-yay par-lay plew lahnt-mahn.*
Je (ne) comprends (pas).	I (do not) understand.	*zhuh (nuh) kawn-prahn (pah).*
Me comprenez-vous ?	Do you understand me?	*muh kawn-pruh-nay-voo ?*
Veuillez répéter, s'il vous plaît.	Repeat it, please.	*vuh-yay ray-pay-tay, seel voo pleh.*
Écrivez-le, s'il vous plaît.	Write it down, please.	*ay-kree-vay-luh, seel voo pleh.*
Que veut dire ceci ?	What does this mean?	*kuh vuh deer suh-see ?*
De rien.	You are welcome.	*duh ree-en.*
Comment dit-on "xx" en français ?	How do you say "xx" in French?	*kaw-mahn dee-tawn "x" ehn frahn-seh ?*
Comment épelez-vous "xx" ?	How do you spell "xx"?	*kaw-mahn tay-play-voo "x" ?*
Qu'est-ce que c'est que ça ?	What is that?	*kes-kuh seh kuh sa ?*

Listen to Track 14

Non.	No.	*noñ.*
Pardon.	Excuse me.	*par-down.*
Peut-être.	Perhaps.	*puh-TEH-truh.*
Oui.	Yes.	*Wee.*

Je suis américain.	I am American.	*zhuh swee za-may-ree-kang.*
Mon adresse est XX.	My address is XX.	*maw na-dress eh XX.*
Que désirez-vous ?	What do you wish?	*kuh Day-zee-ray-voo ?*
Venez ici.	Come here.	*vuh-nay zee-see.*
Entrez.	Come in.	*ahn-tray.*
Attendez un moment.	Wait a moment.	*at-tahn-day zûhn mo-mahn.*

Listen to Track 15

Je suis pressé.	I am in a hurry.	*zhuh swee pres-say.*
J'ai chaud / froid.	I am warm / cold.	*zhay shoh / frwah.*
J'ai faim / soif.	I am hungry / thirsty.	*zhay fen / swahf.*
Je suis occupé / fatigué.	I am busy / tired.	*zhuh swee zaw-kew-pay, fa-tee-gay.*
Je suis content.	I am glad.	*zhahn swee kawn-tahn.*
Je regrette.	I am sorry.	*zhuh ruh-gret.*
Qu'y a-t-il ?	What is the matter here?	*kee a-teel ?*
C'est bien.	It is all right.	*seh byen.*
Je (ne) sais (pas).	I (do not) know.	*zhuh (nuh) say (pah).*
Je (ne) le crois (pas).	I (do not) think so.	*zhuh (nuh) luh krwah (pah).*

Listen to Track 16

Ça ne fait rien.	It doesn't matter.	*sa nuh feh ree-en.*
Combien est-ce ?	How much is it?	*kaum-byen ess ?*
C'est tout.	That is all.	*seh too.*
Pouvez-vous m'aider (me dire) ?	Can you help me (tell me)?	*poo-veah-voo may-day (muh deer) ?*
Où sont les lavabos ?	Where is the washroom?	*oo sawn lay la-va-boh ?*
les toilettes pour hommes	the men's room	*lay twa·let poor om*
les toilettes pour femmes	the ladies room	*lay twa·let poor fam*
Je cherche mon hôtel.	I am looking for my hotel.	*zhuh shehrsh maw no-tel.*
Je voudrais y aller à pied.	I would like to walk there.	*zhuh voo-dreh zee al-lay ah pyay.*
Pourquoi ?	Why?	*poor-kwah ?*

Listen to Track 17

Quand ?	When?	*kahn ?*
Qui ?	Who?	*kee ?*
Quoi ?	What?	*kwah ?*
Comment ?	How?	*kaw-mahn ?*
Combien de temps ?	How long?	*kawn-byen duh tahn ?*
À quelle distance ?	How far?	*ah kel deess-tahns ?*
ici	here	*ee-see*

là	there	*lah*
à	to	*ah*
de	from	*duh*
avec	with	*a-vek*
sans	without	*sahn*
dans	in	*dahn*
sur	on	*sewr*
près de	near	*preh duh*
loin de	far	*iwen duh*

Listen to Track 18

devant	in front of	*duh-vahm*
derrière	behind	*day-ryehr*
à côté de	beside	*ah koh-tay duh*
à l'intérieur	inside	*ah len-tay-ryuhr*
à l'extérieur	outside	*ah lex-tay-ryuhr*
vide	empty	*veed*
plein	full	*pluhn*
quelque chose	something	*kel-kuh shohz*
rien	nothing	*ree-en*
plusieurs	several	*plewzyuhr*

Listen to Track 19

quelques	few	*kel-kuh*
(beaucoup) plus	(much) more	*(boh-koo) plewss*
moins	less	*mwen*
(un peu) plus	(a little) more	*(uhn puh) plewss*

24

assez	enough	*as-say*
trop	too much	*troh*
beaucoup	many	*boh-koo*
bon	good	*bawn*
meilleur (que)	better (than)	*may-yuhr (kuh)*
le meilleur	the best	*luh may-yuhr*

Listen to Track 20

mauvais	bad	*moh-vay*
pire (que)	worse (than)	*peer (kuh)*
maintenant	now	*ment-nahn*
tout de suite	immediately	*toot sweet*
bientôt	soon	*byen-toh*
plus tard	later	*plew tahr*
le plus tôt possible	as soon as possible	*luh plew toh paw-see- bluh*
Il est (trop) tard.	It is (too) late.	*eeleh (troh) tahr.*
Il est tôt.	It is early.	*eel eh toh.*
lentement	slowly	*lanhtuh-mahn*

Listen to Track 21

plus lentement	slower	*plew lahntuh-mahn*
vite	quickly	*veet*
plus vite	faster	*plew veet*
Attention !	Look out!	*ah-tahn-syawn !*
Écoutez.	Listen.	*ay-koo-tay.*
Regardez.	Look.	*ruh-gar-day.*

Comprenez-vous ?	Do you understand?	*kom·pre·ney·voo ?*
Que veut dire (XX) ?	What does (XX) mean?	*ke veu deer (XX) ?*
Comment le prononcez-vous ?	How do you pronounce this?	*ko·mon le pro·non·sey voo ?*
Comment est-ce qu'on écrit (bonjour) ?	How do you write (bonjour)?	*ko·mon es kon ey·kree (bon·zhoor) ?*

Chapter 1.2: Difficulties / Rencontrer des difficultés

Listen to Track 22

Je ne peux pas trouver l'adresse de mon hôtel.	I cannot find my hotel address.	*zhuh nuh puh pah troo-vay la-dress duh maw no-ttel.*
J'ai perdu mes amis.	I have lost my friends.	*zhay pehr-dew may za-mee.*
J'ai laissé mon sac / mon portefeuille à l'hôtel.	I left my purse / wallet in the hotel.	*zhay lay-say mawn sahk, mawn pawrt-Foo-yuh ah lo-tel.*
J'ai oublié mon argent / mes clés.	I forgot my money / keys.	*zhay oo-blee-ay maw nar-zhahn, may klay.*
J'ai manqué mon train.	I have missed my train.	*zhay mahn-kay mawn tren.*
Que dois-je faire ?	What am I to do?	*kuh DWAH-zhuh fehr ?*
Mes lunettes sont cassées.	My glasses are broken.	*may lew-net sawn kas-say.*
Où peut-on les faire réparer ?	Where can they be repaired?	*oo puh-tawn lay fehr ray-pa-ray ?*
un appareil auditif	a hearing aid	*uh nap-pa-ray a-kooss teek*
le bureau des objets trouvés	the lost and found desk	*luh bew-roh day zawb-zheh troo-vay*

Listen to Track 23

le consulat des États-Unis	the American consulate	luh kawn-sew-la day zay-ta-zew-nee
le commissariat de police	the police station	luh kaw-mee-sa-rya duh paw-leess
Je vais appeler un agent.	I will call a policeman.	zhuh vay za-play uh na-zhahn.
On m'a volé.	I've been robbed.	on ma vo·ley.
J'ai perdu ...	I've lost my ...	zhey pair·dew
... on m'a vole.	... was/were stolen.	... on ma vo·ley.
... mon sac à dos	... my backpack	... mon sak a do
... mes valises	... my bags	... mey va·leez
... ma carte de credit	... my credit card	... ma kart de krey·dee
... mon sac à main	... my handbag	... mon sak a mun

Listen to Track 24

... mes bijoux	... my jewellery	... mey bee·zhoo
... mon argent	... my money	... mon ar·zhon
... mon passeport	... my passport	... mom pas·por
... mes chèques de voyage	... my traveler's cheques	... mey shek de vwa·yazh

... **mon portefeuille**	... my wallet	... *mom por·te·feu·ye*
Je veux contacter mon ...	I want to contact my ...	*zhuh veu kon·tak·tey mon*
... **consulat**	... consulate	... *kon·sew·la*
... **ambassade**	... embassy	... *om·ba·sad*

Chapter 2: Talking to people / S'adresser aux autres

Chapter 2.1: Social interaction / Les interactions sociales

The main point of speaking French is to use the language in everyday conversation. As intimidating as it can be to converse in a different language, this is the ultimate goal of your studies. It is a good idea to have some basic phrases up your sleeve for when you are having conversations with people in French. These handy conversation starters and tips are ideal for those times when you need something relevant to say to keep the dialogue going.

Listen to Track 25

Oui, merci.	Yes, please.	_wee, mehr-see._
Non, merci.	No, thanks.	_noñ, mehr-see._
D'accord !	Ok!	_da-kor !_
Monsieur/M.	Sir/Mr.	_muh-syuh._
Madame/Mme.	Madam/Mrs./Ms.	_ma-dam._
Mademoiselle/ Mlle	Miss	_mad-mwa-zel_
Bonjour ! / Salut !	Hello! / Hi!	_boñ-zhoor ! / sa-lew !_
À bientôt.	Bye for now.	_a byañ-toh._
Bonsoir.	Good evening.	_boñ-swar._
Bonne nuit.	Goodnight.	_bon nwee._

Listen to Track 26

| À demain. | See you tomorrow. | _a duh-mañ._ |

Pardon, monsieur/ madame !	Excuse me, sir/ madam! (to catch attention)	*par-doñ, muh-syuh/ma-dam !*
Je suis désolé(e).	I'm sorry.	*zhuh swee day-zo-lay.*
Comment allez-vous ?	How are you?	*ko-mahñ ta-lay voo ?*
Très bien, merci.	Fine, thanks.	*treh byañ, mehr-see.*
Et vous ?	And you?	*ay voo ?*
Est-ce que je peux ...	Can I ...	*es kuh zhuh puh ...*
... fumer ?	... smoke?	*... few-may ?*
Le repas était délicieux.	The meal was delicious.	*luh ruh-pa ay-teh day-lee-syuh.*
Je vous remercie.	Thank you very much.	*zhuh voo ruh-mehr-see.*

Listen to Track 27

Enchanté(e) !	Delighted to meet you!	*ahñ-shahñ-tay !*
Voici ...	This is ...	*vwa-see ...*
... mon mari/ ma femme.	... my husband/ my wife.	*... moñ ma-ree/ ma fam.*
Passez de bonnes vacances !	Enjoy your holiday!	*pa-say duh bon va-kahñs !*
Quel est votre (politesse) / Quel est ton (informel) ...	What's your ...	*kel ey vo·tre / kel ey ton ...*
... adresse ?	... address?	*... a·dress ?*

... e-mail ?	... email address?	... ey·mel ?
... numéro de téléphone ?	... phone number?	... new·mey·ro de tehlehfohn ?

Listen to Track 28

Vous venez d'où ? (politesse)	Where are you from?	voo ve·ney doo ?
Tu viens d'où ? (informel)	Where are you from?	tew vyun do o ?
Je viens ...	I'm from ...	zhe vyun ...
... d'Australie.	... Australia.	... dos·tra·lee.
... du Canada.	... Canada.	... dew ka·na·da.
... d'Angleterre.	... England.	... dong·gle· tair.
... de Nouvelle-Zélande.	... New Zealand.	... de noo·vel· zey·lond.
... des Etats-Unis.	... the USA.	... dey.

Listen to Track 29

Est-ce que vous êtes marié(e) ? m/f (politesse)	Are you married?	es·ke voo zet mar·yey ?
Est-ce que tu es marié(e) ? m/f (informel)	Are you married?	es·ke tew ey mar·yey ?

Je suis marié/ mariée. m/f	I'm married.	*zhe swee mar·yey.*
Je suis célibataire.	I'm single.	*zhe swee sey·lee·ba·tair.*
Quel âge	How old ...	*kel azh ...*
... avez-vous ? (politesse)	... are you?	*...a·vey·voo ?*
... as-tu ... ? (informel)	... are you?	*... a·tew ?*
... a votre fille ? (politesse)	... is your daughter?	*... a vo·tre fee·ye ?*
... a votre fils ? (politesse)	... is your son?	*... a vo·tre fees ?*
J'ai ... ans.	I'm ... years old.	*zhey ... on.*
Il/Elle a ... ans.	He/She is ... years old.	*eel/el a ... on.*
Je (ne) suis (pas)...	I'm (not) ...	*zhe (ne) swee (pa) ...*

Listen to Track 30

Êtes-vous ... (politesse)	Are you ...	*et voo ...*
Es·tu (informel)	Are you ...	*Ey-tew ...*
... le petit ami de ?	... the boyfriend?	*... le pe-tee ta-mee ?*
... le frère de ?	... the brother?	*... le frair de ?*
... la fille de ?	... the daughter?	*... la fee-ye ?*
... le père de ?	... the father?	*... le pair de ?*

... l'ami/amie m/f de ?	... the friend?	... la-mee de ?
... la petite amie de ?	... the girlfriend?	... la pe-teet a-mee de?
... le mari de ?	... the husband?	... le ma-ree de ?
... la mère de ?	... the mother?	... la mair de ?
... le/la partenaire de ?	... the partner?	... le/la par-te-nair de ?
... la sœur de ?	... the sister?	... la seur de ?
... le fils de ?	... the son?	... le fees de ?
... la femme de ?	... the wife?	... la fam de ?

Listen to Track 31

Voici ...	Here's ...	vwa-see ...
... mon frère.	... my brother.	... mawn frehr.
... mon ami.	... my friend.	... maw na-mee.
... ma femme.	... my wife.	... mafahm.
... mon mari.	... my husband.	... mawn ma-ree.
... ma sœur.	... my sister.	... ma suhr.
... ma fille.	... my daughter.	... ma fee-yuh.
... mon fils.	... my son.	... mawn fees.
... mon enfant.	... my child.	... maw nahn-fahn.

Listen to Track 32

le garçon	the boy	*luh gar-sawn*
la jeune fille	the girl	*la zhuhn fee-yuh*
l'homme	the man	*lawm*
la femme	the woman	*lafahm*
heureux/ heureuse m/f	happy	*er-reu/er-reuz*
triste	sad	*treest*
froid/froide m/f	cold	*frwa/frwad*
chaud/chaude m/f	hot	*sho/shod*
J'ai faim.	I am hungry.	*fum*
J'ai soif.	I am thirsty.	*swaf*

Listen to Track 33

Pourriez-vous ...	Could you ...	*poo-ree-yey voo ...*
S'il vous plait ...	Please ...	*seel voo pley ...*
... répéter ?	... repeat?	*... rey-pey-tey ?*
Je vous souhaite ...	I'd like to wish you ...	*zhuh voo soo-eht ...*
... une Bonne Année !	... a Happy New Year!	*... bon a-nay !*
... de joyeuses Pâques !	... a Happy Easter!	*... de zhwa-yuz pak !*
... un bon anniversaire !	... a Happy Birthday!	*... boñ na-nee-vehr-sehr !*

Bon voyage !	Have a good trip!	*boñ vwa-yazh !*
Bon appétit !	Enjoy your meal!	*boñ na-pay-tee !*
Comment tu t'appelles?	What's your name?	*ko-mahñ tew ta-pel ?*
Je m'appelle ...	My name is ...	*zhuh ma-pel ...*
Tu es d'où ?	Where are you from?	*tew ay doo ?*
Je suis anglais(e), de Londres.	I am English, from London.	*zhuh swee zahñ-gleh(z), duh loñdr.*
Enchanté(e) !	Pleased to meet you!	*on-shon-tay !*

Chapter 2.2: Get to know somebody / Faire connaissance avec quelqu'un

Listen to Track 34

Quel âge as-tu ?	How old are you?	*kel azh a tew ?*
J'ai ... ans.	I'm ... years old.	*zhay ... ahñ.*
Tu es français(e) ?	Are you French?	*tew ay frahñ-seh(z) ?*
Je suis anglais(e)/ écossais(e)/ américain(e).	I'm English/ Scottish/ American.	*zhuh swee zong-gley (z)/ zay-koseh(z)/za-mayree-kañ/ken.*
Où est-ce que tu habites ?	Where do you live?	*oo es kuh tew a-beet ?*
Où est-ce que vous habitez ?	*Where do you live?*	*oo es kuh voo za-bee-tay ?*
J'habite à Londres.	I live in London.	*zha-beet a loñdr.*
Nous habitons à Glasgow.	We live in Glasgow.	*noo za-bee-toñ a glaz-goh.*

Listen to Track 35

Je suis ...	I'm ...	*zhuh swee ...*
... célibataire.	... single.	*... say-lee-ba-tehr.*
... marié(e).	... married.	*... mar-yay.*
... divorcé(e).	... divorced.	*... dee-vor-say.*
J'ai ...	I have ...	*zhay ...*
... un petit ami.	... a boyfriend.	*... uñ puh-tee-ta-mee.*

... une petite amie.	... a girlfriend.	*... ewn puh-teet a-mee.*
J'ai un compagnon/ une compagne.	I have a partner (male/female).	*zhay uñ kom-pa-nyoñ/ewn koñ-panyuh.*
J'ai ... enfants.	I have ... children.	*zhay ahñ-fahñ.*
Je n'ai pas d'enfants.	I have no children.	*zhuh nay pas dahñ-fahñ.*
Je suis ici en vacances/ en voyage d'affaires/ en week-end.	I'm here on holiday/on business/for the weekend.	*zhuh swee zee-see ahñ va-kahñs/ ahñ vwa-yazh da-fehr/ahñ wee-kend.*
Qu'est-ce que vous faites comme travail ?	What work do you do?	*kes kuh voo fet kom tra-va-yuh ?*

Listen to Track 36

Je suis ...	I'm ...	*zhuh swee ...*
... médecin.	... a doctor.	*... may-dsañ.*
... directeur.	... a manager.	*... dee-rek-tur.*
... secrétaire.	... a secretary.	*... suh-kray-tehr.*
Je travaille à domicile.	I work from home.	*zhuh tra-va-yuh a do-mee-seel.*
Je travaille à mon compte.	I'm self-employed.	*zhuh tra-va-yuh a moñ koñt.*

Chapter 3: On the go: Direction and transportation / En déplacement : Direction et transport

There is nothing worse than feeling lost, let alone being lost in a foreign country. Learning French has, of course, some very practical uses when you are in a French speaking country. When traveling, having a basic understanding of how to ask for directions or simply knowing the words for public transportation can make all the difference in your experience.

Chapter 3.1: Asking for direction / Demander son chemin

Listen to Track 37

en face de	opposite of	*ahñ fas duh*
à côté de	next to	*a ko-tay duh*
près de	near to	*preh duh*
le carrefour	the crossroad	*luh kar-foor*
le rond-point	the roundabout	*luh roñ-pwañ*
Pardon, pour aller à la gare ? (Excusez-moi, comment puis-je aller à la gare ?)	Excuse me, how do I get to the station?	*par-doñ, poor a-lay a la gar ?*
Continuez tout droit, après l'église tournez à gauche/à droite.	Keep straight on, after the church turn left/right.	*koñ-tee-new-ay too drwa, a-preh lay-gleez toor-nay a gohsh/a drwat.*
C'est loin ?	Is it far?	*say lwañ ?*

Non, c'est à deux cents mètres/à cinq minutes.	No, 200 yards/ five minutes.	*noñ, say ta duh sahñ metr/a sañk mee-newt.*

Listen to Track 38

Nous cherchons ...	We're looking for ...	*noo shehr-shoñ ...*
On peut y aller à pied ?	Can we walk there?	*oñ puh ee a-lay a pyay ?*
Nous nous sommes perdu(e)s.	We're lost.	*noo noo som pehr-dew.*
C'est la bonne direction pour... ?	Is this the right way to...?	*say la bon dee-rek-syoñ poor... ?*
Pouvez-vous me montrer sur la carte ?	Can you show me on the map?	*poo-vay voo me moñ-tray sewr la kart ?*
C'est indiqué.	It's signposted.	*say tañ-dee-kay.*
C'est au coin de la rue.	It's on the corner of the street.	*say toh kwañ duh la rew.*
C'est là-bas.	It's over there.	*say la-ba.*

Chapter 3.2: Taking the bus and coach / Prendre le bus et le car

Listen to Track 39

Pardon, quel bus pour le centre-ville ? (Pardon, quel bus va au centre-ville ?)	Excuse me, which bus goes to the center?	*par-doñ, kel bews poor luh sahñtr veel ?*
Le 10.	Number 10.	*luh deess.*
Où est l'arrêt ?	Where is the bus stop?	*oo ay la-reh ?*
Là-bas, à gauche.	There, on the left.	*la-ba, a gohsh.*
Où est-ce que je peux acheter des tickets de bus ?	Where can I buy bus tickets?	*oo es kuh zhuh puh ash-tay day tee-keh duh bews ?*
Là-bas, au distributeur.	Over there, at the ticket machine.	*la-ba, oh dees-tree-bew-tur.*
Est-ce qu'il y a un bus pour... ?	Is there a bus to...?	*es keel ya uñ bews poor... ?*
Où est-ce qu'on prend le bus pour aller à/au ... ?	Where do I catch the bus to go to...?	*oo es koñ prahñ luh bews poor a-lay a/oh... ?*

Listen to Track 40

C'est combien pour aller... (Combien ça coûte pour aller ...)	How much is it to go ...	*say koñ-byañ poor a-lay a/oh*
... au centre ?	... to the center?	*... oh sahñtr ?*
... à la plage ?	... to the beach?	*... a la plazh ?*
... aux magasins ?	... to the shops?	*... oh ma-ga-zañ ?*
... à Montmartre ?	... to Montmartre?	*... a moñ-martr ?*
Les bus pour ... passent tous les combien de temps ?	How frequent are the buses to...?	*lay bews poor ... pas too lay koñ-byañ duh tahñ ?*
À quelle heure part le premier/le dernier bus pour... ?	When is the first/ the last bus to...?	*a kel ur par luh pruh-myay/ luh dehr-nyay bews poor... ?*
Pourriez-vous me dire quand descender ?	Could you tell me when to get off?	*poo-ree-ay-voo muh deer kahñ deh-sahñdr ?*
C'est mon arrêt.	This is my stop.	*say moñ na-reh.*
Prenez le métro, c'est plus rapide.	Take the metro, it's quicker.	*pruh-nay luh may-troh, say plew ra-peed.*

Chapter 3.3: Taking the metro / Prendre le métro

Listen to Track 41

entrée	entrance	_ahñ-tray_
sortie	way out/exit	_sor-tee_
la ligne de métro	metro line	_la lee-nyuh duh may-troh_
en direction de	in the direction of	_ahñ dee-rek-syoñ duh_
correspondance	connecting line	_ko-res-poñ-dahñs_
Où est la station de métro la plus proche ?	Where is the nearest metro?	_oo ay la sta-syoñ duh may-troh la plew prosh ?_
Je vais à ...	I'm going to ...	_zhuh veh a ..._
Comment marche le guichet automatique ?	How does the ticket machine work?	_ko-mahñ marsh luh gee-sheh oh-toh-ma-teek ?_
Vous avez un plan du metro ?	Do you have a map of the metro?	_voo za-vay uñ plahñ dew may-troh ?_
Pour aller à/au... ? (Pourriez-vous me dire comment aller à/au ... ?)	How do I get to ...? (Please tell me how I get to ...?)	_poor a-lay a/oh... ?_
Est-ce qu'il faut changer ?	Do I have to change?	_es keel foh shañ-zhay ?_
C'est quelle ligne pour... ?	Which line is it for...?	_say kel lee-nyuh poor... ?_

Dans quelle direction ?	In which direction?	*dahñ kel dee-rek-syoñ ?*
Quel est le prochain arrêt ?	What is the next stop?	*kel ay luh pro-shañ na-reh ?*

Chapter 3.4: Traveling by train / Voyager en train

Listen to Track 42

l'horaire	the timetable	*lo-rehr*
circuler	to operate	*seer-kew-lay*
Dimanches et fêtes	Sundays and holidays	*dee-mahñsh ay fet*
accès aux quais	access to the platforms	*ak-seh oh keh*
Quand part le prochain train pour... ?	When is the next train to...?	*kahñ par luh pro-shañ trañ poor ?*
A 17 heures 10.	At ten past five.	*a dee-set ur dees.*
Deux billets pour ...	Two tickets to ...	*duh bee-yeh poor ...*
Aller simple ou aller-retour ?	Single or return?	*a-lay sañpl oo a-lay-ruh-toor ?*
première classe / deuxième classe	first class / second class	*pruh myehr klas / duh-zyem klas*
fumeur/non fumeur	smoking / non-smoking	*few-mur / noñ few-mur*

Listen to Track 43

Y a-t-il un supplément à payer ?	Is there a supplement to pay?	*ee a-teel uñ sew-play-mahñ a payyay ?*
Je voudrais réserver une place dans le TGV pour Nîmes.	I want to book a seat on the TGV to Nîmes.	*zhuh voo-dreh ray-zehr-vay ewn plas dahñ luh tay-zhay-vay poor neem.*

Le train pour ... est à quelle heure ?	When is the train to...?	*luh trañ poor ay ta kel ur ?*
le premier / le dernier	the first / the last	*luh pruh myay / luh dehr-nyay*
À quelle heure arrive-t-il à... ?	When does it arrive in...?	*a kel ur a-reev-teel a... ?*
Est-ce qu'il faut changer ?	Do I have to change?	*es keel foh shañ-zhay ?*
Il part de quel quai ?	Which platform does it leave from?	*eel par duh kel kay ?*
C'est le bon quai pour le train pour Paris ?	Is this the right platform for the train to Paris?	*say luh boñ kay poor luh trañ duh pa-ree ?*
C'est le train pour... ?	Is this the train for...?	*say luh trañ poor... ?*
Il part à quelle heure ?	When does it leave?	*eel par a kel ur ?*
Est-ce que le train s'arrête à... ?	Does the train stop at...?	*es kuh luh trañ sa-ret a... ?*
Où dois-je changer pour... ?	Where do I change for...?	*oo dwa-zhuh shahñ-zhay poor... ?*
S'il vous plaît, prévenez-moi quand nous serons à ...	Please tell me when we get to ...	*seel voo pleh, pray-vnay mwa kañ noo suh-roñ za ...*
Cette place est-elle libre ?	Is this seat free?	*set plas ay-tel leebr ?*

Chapter 3.5: Taking a taxi / Prendre le taxi

Listen to Track 44

la station de taxis	the taxi rank	*la sta-syoñ duh tak-see*
Je voudrais un taxi.	I want a taxi.	*zhuh voo-dreh uñ tak-see.*
Où est-ce que je peux prendre un taxi ?	Where can I get a taxi?	*oo es kuh zhuh puh prahñdr uñ tak-see ?*
Pouvez-vous m'appeler un taxi ?	Could you order me a taxi?	*poo-vay voo ma-play uñ tak-see ?*
Combien ça va coûter pour aller ...	How much is it going to cost to go ...	*koñ-byañ sa va koo-tay poor a-lay a/oh ...*
... au centre-ville ?	... to the town center?	*... oh sahñtr-veel ?*
... à la gare ?	... to the station?	*... a la gar ?*
... à l'aéroport ?	... to the airport?	*... a la-ay-ro-por ?*
... à cette adresse ?	... to this address?	*... a set a-dres ?*
C'est combien ?	How much is it?	*say koñ-byañ ?*
C'est plus qu'au compteur.	It's more than on the meter.	*say plew skoh koñ-tur.*
Gardez la monnaie.	Keep the change.	*gar-day la mo-neh.*
Je suis désolé(e), je n'ai pas de monnaie.	Sorry, I don't have any change.	*zhuh swee day-zo-lay, zhuh nay pa duh mo-neh.*
Je suis pressé(e).	I'm in a hurry.	*zhuh swee preh-say.*
C'est loin ?	Is it far?	*say lwañ ?*

Chapter 3.6: Traveling by boat and ferry / Voyager en bateau et bac

Listen to Track 45

À quelle heure part le prochain bateau/ferry pour ... ?	When is the next boat/ferry to ...?	*a kel ur par luh pro-shañ ba-toh/ feh-ree poor ... ?*
Vous avez un horaire ?	Do you have a timetable?	*voo za-vay uñ noh-rehr ?*
Est-ce qu'il y a un car ferry (transbordeur) pour ... ?	Is there a car ferry to ...?	*es keel ya uñ car feh-ree poor ... ?*
C'est combien ...	How much is ...	*seh koñ-byañ ...*
... pour un aller simple ?	... a single (one-way)?	*... uñ na-lay sañpl ?*
... pour un aller-retour ?	... a return (round trip)?	*... uñ na-lay-ruh-toor ?*
... un billet touristique ?	... a tourist ticket?	*... uñ bee-yeh too-rees-teek ?*
C'est combien pour une voiture et ... personnes ?	How much is it for a car and ... people?	*say koñ-byañ poor ewn vwa-tewr ay ... pehr-son ?*
La traversée dure combien de temps ?	How long is the crossing?	*la tra-vehr-say dewr koñ-byañ duh tahñ ?*
D'où part le bateau ?	Where does the boat leave from?	*doo par luh ba-toh ?*

Le premier/ dernier bateau part quand ?	When is the first/ last boat?	*luh pruh-myay/ dehr-nyay ba-toh par kahñ ?*
On arrive à quelle heure à … ?	What time do we get to …?	*on a-reev a kel ur a … ?*
Est-ce qu'on peut manger sur le bateau ?	Is there somewhere to eat on the boat?	*es koñ puh mahñ-zhay sewr luh batoh ?*

Chapter 3.7: Air travel / Le transport aérien

Listen to Track 46

Comment fait-on pour aller à l'aéroport ?	How do I get to the airport?	*ko-mahñ fay toñ poor a-lay a la-ay-ro-por ?*
On met combien de temps pour aller à l'aéroport ?	How long does it take to get to the airport?	*oñ meh koñ-byañ duh tahñ poor a-lay a la-ay-ro-por ?*
C'est combien le taxi pour aller ...	How much is the taxi fare ...	*say koñ-byañ luh tak-see poor alay ...*
... en ville ?	... into town?	*... ahñ veel ?*
... à l'hôtel ?	... to the hotel?	*... a loh-tel ?*
Est-ce qu'il y a une navette pour aller au centre-ville ?	Is there an airport bus to the city center?	*es keel ya ewn na-vet poor a-lay oh sahñtr-veel ?*
Où est l'enregistrement pour ... ?	Where do I check in for ...?	*oo ay lahñ-ruh-zhee-struh-mahñ poor ... ?*
Où sont les bagages du vol en provenance de ... ?	Where is the luggage for the flight from ...?	*oo soñ lay ba-gazh dew vol ahñ pro-vnahñs duh ... ?*
Quelle est la porte d'embarquement pour le vol à destination de ... ?	Which is the departure gate for the flight to ...?	*kel ay la port dahñ-bar-kuh-mahñ poor luh vol a des-tee-na-syoñ duh ... ?*

L'embarquement aura lieu porte numéro ...	Boarding will take place at gate number ...	*lahñ-bar-kuh-mahñ oh-ra lyuh port new-may-ro ...*
Présentez-vous immédiatement porte numéro ...	Go immediately to gate number ...	*pray-zahñ-tay voo ee-maydyatmahñ port new-may-ro ...*
Votre vol a du retard.	Your flight is delayed.	*votr vol a dew ruh-tar.*

Chapter 3.8: Customs control / Les douanes

Listen to Track 47

contrôle des passeports	passport control	*koñ-trol day pas-por*
UE (Union Européenne)	EU (European Union)	*ew uh*
autres passeports	other passports	*ohtr pas-por*
douane	customs	*doo-an*
Est-ce que je dois payer des droits de douane sur ça ?	Do I have to pay duty on this?	*es kuh zhuh dwa pay-yay day drwa duh dwan sewr sa ?*
C'est pour mon usage personnel.	It is for my own personal use.	*say poor moñ new-zazh pehr-so-nel.*
Nous allons en/au/aux ...	We are on our way to ... (if in transit through a country)	*noo za-loñ ahñ/ oh/oh ...*

Chapter 3.9: Petrol, gas / Les carburants

Listen to Track 48

sans plomb	unleaded	_sahñ ploñ_
diesel/gasoil	diesel	_dee-eh-zel/ ga-zwal_
Le plein, s'il vous plaît.	Fill it up, please.	_luh plañ, seel voo pleh._
Pouvez-vous vérifier l'huile/ l'eau ?	Can you check the oil/the water?	_poo-vay voo vay-ree-fyay lweel/ loh ?_
Euros d'essence sans plomb.	Euros' worth of unleaded petrol.	_uh-roh deh-sahñs sahñ ploñ._
La pompe numéro ...	Pump number ...	_la pomp new-may-roh ..._
Pouvez-vous vérifier la pression des pneus ?	Can you check the tire pressure?	_Poo-vay voo vay-ree-fyay la preh-syoñ day pnuh ?_
Où dois-je payer ?	Where do I pay?	_oo dwa-zhuh pay-yay ?_
Vous acceptez les cartes de credit ?	Do you take credit cards?	_voo zak-sep-tay lay kart duh kray-dee ?_

Chapter 3.10: Car breakdown / Panne de voiture

Listen to Track 49

Une assistance automobile.	A breakdown assistance.	*a-sees-tahñs oh-toh-mo-beel.*
Pouvez-vous m'aider ?	Can you help me?	*poo-vay voo may-day ?*
Ma voiture est en panne.	My car has broken down.	*ma vwa-tewr ay tahñ pan.*
Je n'arrive pas à démarrer.	I can't start the car.	*zhuh na-reev pa a day-ma-ray.*
Je suis en panne d'essence.	I've run out of petrol.	*zhuh swee ahñ pan deh-sahñs.*
Il y a un garage près d'ici ?	Is there a garage near here?	*eel ya uñ ga-razh preh dee-see ?*
Pouvez-vous me remorquer jusqu'au garage le plus proche ?	Can you tow me to the nearest garage?	*poo-vay voo muh ruh-mor-kay zhew-skoh ga-razh luh plew prosh ?*
Avez-vous des pièces de rechange pour une ... ?	Do you have parts for a ...? (make of car)	*a-vay voo day pyes duh ruh-shahñzh poor ewn ... ?*
J'ai un problème avec le/la/les ...	There's something wrong with the ...	*zhay uñ prob-lem a-vek luh/la/lay ...*

Chapter 3.11: Car parts / Les pièces détachées

Listen to Track 50

Le/La/L' ... ne marche pas.	The ... doesn't work.	_luh/la/l ... nuh marsh pa._
Les ... ne marchent pas.	The ... don't work.	_lay ... nuh marsh pa._
l'accélérateur	accelerator	_lak-say-lay-ra-tur_
la batterie	battery	_la ba-tree_
le capot	bonnet	_luh ka-poh_
les freins	brakes	_leh frañ_
le starter	choke	_luh star-tehr_
l'embrayage	clutch	_lahñ-bray-yazh_
le delco	distributor	_luh del-koh_
le moteur	engine	_luh mo-tur_
le pot d'échappement	exhaust pipe	_luh poh day-shapmahñ_
le fusible	fuse	_luh few-zeebl_
les vitesses	gears	_lay vee-tes_
le frein à main	handbrake	_luh frañ a mañ_
les phares	headlights	_lay far_
l'allumage	ignition	_la-lew-mazh_

Listen to Track 51

le clignotant	indicator	_luh klee-nyo-tahñ_
les vis platinées	points	_lay vees pla-tee-nay_
le radiateur	radiator	_luh ra-dya-tur_
les feux de recul	reversing lights	_lay far duh ruh-kewl_

la ceinture de sécurité	seat belt	*la sañ-tewr duh say-kewr-eetay*
les feux de position	sidelights	*lay vay-yuhz*
la roue de secours	spare wheel	*la roo duh skoor*
les bougies	spark plugs	*lay boo-zhee*
la direction	steering	*la dee-rek-syoñ*
le volant	steering wheel	*luh vo-lahñ*
le pneu	tyre	*luh pnuh*
la roue	wheel	*la roo*
le pare-brise	windscreen (windshield)	*luh par-breez*
le lave-glace	windscreen washer (windshield washer)	*luh lav-glas*
l'essuie-glace	windscreen wiper (windshield wiper)	*les-wee-glas*

Chapter 3.12: Road signs / La signalisation routière

Listen to Track 52

douane zoll	customs	*dwan zoll*
halte peage	toll station for motorway	*al-tuh pai-ah-zhuh*
cédez le passage	give way	*say-day luh pah-sahzh*
ralentir	slow down	*ra-lon-teer*
sens unique	one way	*sahns oo-neek*
déviation	detour	*dai-vee-a-see-on*
nord	north	*nor*
sud	south	*sood*
ouest	west	*oo-aist*
est	east	*aist*
libre	spaces	*lee-bruh*
complet	full	*kom-play*
stationnement interdit	no parking	*sta-see-on-mon an-tair-dee*
allumez vos feux	switch on your light	*ay-loo-may voh fuh*
autoroute	motorway	*o-toe-root*

Chapter 3.13: Signs and notices / Les panneaux

Listen to Track 53

entrée	entrance	*on-tray*
sortie	exit	*sor-tee*
ouvert	open	*oo-vair*
fermé	closed	*fair-may*
chaud	hot	*sho*
froid	cold	*frwa*
tirez	pull	*tee-ray*
poussez	push	*poo-say*
à droite	right	*ah drwat*
à gauche	left	*ah gosh*
eau potable	drinking water	*o po-tah-bluh*
à emporter	take-away	*ah on-por-tay*
dégustation de vin	wine tasting	*day-goos-tah-sion duh vahng*

Listen to Track 54

libre	free, vacant	*lee-bruh*
occupé	engaged/occupied	*o-koo-pay*
caisse	cash desk	*kess*
libre-service	self-service	*lee-bruh sair-vees*
toilettes	toilets	*twa-let*
dames	ladies (women)	*dam*
hommes, messieurs	gents (men)	*om, may-syuh*
hors service	out of order	*or sair-vees*
à louer	for hire/to rent	*ah loo-ay*

à vendre	for sale	*ah von-druh*
soldes	sale	*sol-duh*
baignade interdite	no bathing	*bae-nyad an-tair-deet*
sous-sol	basement	*soo-sol*
rez-de-chaussée	ground floor	*ray-duh-shoh-say*
ascenseur	lift	*ah-son-suhr*
accès aux trains	*access to the trains*	*ak-say o tran*

Listen to Track 55

chambres disponibles	rooms available	*shon-bruh*
complet	no vacancies	*kon-play*
sortie de secours	emergency exit	*sor-tee duh suh-koor*
sonnez	ring	*soh-nay*
appuyez	press	*ah-pwee-yay*
privé	private	*pree-vay*
arrêt	stop	*ah-ray*
billets	tickets	*bee-yay*
accueil	information	*ah-kuh-yuh*
compostez votre billet	validate your ticket	*kom-pos-tay voh-truh bee-yay*
buffet	snacks	*boo-fay*
consigne	left luggage	*kon-see-nyuh*
non fumeurs / défense de fumer	non-smoking / no smoking	*non foo-muhr / day-fons duh foo-may*
fumeurs	smoking	*foomuhr*

Chapter 4: Leisure, culture and entertainment / Les loisirs, la culture et le divertissement

One of the wonderful aspects of learning a language is the cultural immersion and the experiences you gain from it. French culture has a wealth of connections to leisure and entertainment, which can really enhance your level of enjoyment when learning the language. When you take your interests, such as sports or the arts, and apply to them to learning French, you will find that you are more motivated and interested in increasing your knowledge about that topic while also learning the language along the way.

Chapter 4.1: Sightseeing and tourist office / L'office de tourisme

Listen to Track 56

Où est l'office de tourisme ?	Where is the tourist office?	*oo eh lo-fees duh too-reesm ?*
Qu'est-ce qu'il y a à voir dans la region ?	What is there to visit in the area?	*kes keel ya a vwar dahñ la ray-zhyoñ ?*
En ... heures.	In ... hours.	*ahñ ur.*
Avez-vous de la documentation ?	Do you have any leaflets?	*a-vay voo duh la do-kew-mahñ-ta-syoñ ?*
Est-ce qu'il y a des excursions ?	Are there any excursions?	*es keel ya day zek-skewr-syoñ ?*
On voudrait aller à ...	We'd like to go to ...	*oñ voo-dreh a-lay a ...*

C'est combien l'entrée? / Combien coûte l'entrée ?	How much does it cost to get in?	*say koñ-byañ lahñ-tray ?*
Est-ce que vous faites des réductions pour ...	Are there any discounts for ...	*es kuh voo feht day ray-dewk-syoñ poor ...*
... les enfants ?	... children?	*... lay zahñ-fahñ ?*
... les étudiants ?	... students?	*... lay zay-tew-dyahñ ?*
... les chômeurs ?	... the unemployed?	*... lay shoh-mur ?*
... les retraités ?	... senior citizens?	*... lay ruh-treh-tay ?*

Listen to Track 57

Je voudrais un guide qui parle anglais.	I want a guide who speaks English.	*zhuh dayzeer uhn gheed kee par lahngleh.*
Quel est le prix de l'heure (de la journée) ?	What is the charge per hour (day)?	*kel eh luh pree duh luhr (duh la zhoor nay) ?*
Je m'intéresse à la peinture.	I am interested in painting.	*zhuh men-tay-ress ah la pentewr.*
... la sculpture	... sculpture	*... la skewl-tewr*
... l'architecture	... architecture	*... larshee-tek-tewr*
... le château	... the castle	*... luh shah-toh*
... la cathédrale	... the cathedral	*... la ka-tay-dral*

... le musée	... the museum	... luh mew-zay
Où est l'entrée, la sortie ?	Where is the entrance, exit?	oo eh lahn-tray, la sawr-tee ?
Quel est le prix d'entrée ?	What is the price of admission?	keh leh luh pree dahn-tray ?

Listen to Track 58

monastère (m)	monastery	mo·na·stair
monument (m)	monument	mo·new·mon
vieille ville (f)	old city	vyey veel
palais (m)	palace	pa·ley
ruines (f) (pl)	ruins	rween
stade (m)	stadium	stad
statues (f) (pl)	statues	sta·tew
place centrale (f)	main square	plas son·tral
château (m)	castle	sha·to
cathédrale (f)	cathedral	ka·tey·dral
église (f)	church	ey·gleez

Listen to Track 59

Quelle est l'heure ...	What time does it ...	kel ey leur ...
... de fermeture ?	... close?	... de fer·me·tewr ?
... d'ouverture ?	... open?	... doo·vair·tewr ?
Quel est le tarif du billet d'entrée ?	What's the admission charge?	kel ey le pree dad·mee·syon ?

Y a-t-il une réduction pour les enfants/ étudiants ?	Is there a discount for children/ students?	*eel ya ewn rey·dewk·syon poor ley zon·fon/ zey·tew·dyon ?*
Je voudrais ...	I'd like ...	*zhe voo·drey*
... un catalogue.	... a catalogue.	*... ung ka·ta·log.*
... un guide.	... a guide.	*... ung geed.*
... une carte de la région.	... a local map.	*... ewn kart de la rey·zhyon.*
J'aimerais voir ...	I'd like to see ...	*zhem·rey vwar ...*
Qu'est-ce que c'est ?	What's that?	*kes·ke sey ?*
Je peux prendre des photos ?	Can I take photos?	*zhe peu pron·dre dey fo·to ?*

Listen to Track 60

C'est quand la prochaine ...	When's the next ...	*sey kon la pro·shen ...*
... excursion ?	... tour?	*... eks·kewr·syon ?*
... excursion d'une journée ?	... day trip excursion?	*... eks·kewr·syon dewn zhoor·ney ?*
Est-ce que ... est inclus/ incluse ?	Is ... included?	*es·ke ... ey tung·klew/ tung·klewz ?*
... le logement (m)	... accommodation	*... le lozh·mon*

... l'accès aux visites, aux excursions (m)	... the admission charge	... lad·mee·syon
... la nourriture	... food	... la noo·ree·tewr
... le transport	... transport	... le trons·por
L'excursion dure combien de temps ?	How long is the tour?	leks·kewr·syon dewr kom·byun de tom ?
On doit rentrer pour quelle heure ?	What time should we be back?	on dwa ron·trey poor kel eur ?

Chapter 4.2: Fun and entertainment / Amusement et divertissement

Listen to Track 61

Qu'est-ce qu'on peut faire le soir ?	What is there to do in the evenings?	*kes koñ puh fehr luh swar ?*
Vous avez une liste des festivités pour ce mois-ci ?	Do you have a list of events for this month?	*Voo za-vay ewn leest day fes-tee-vee-tay poor suh mwa-see ?*
Est-ce qu'il y a des choses à faire pour les enfants ?	Is there anything for children to do?	*es keel ya day shohz a fehr poor lay zahñ-fahñ ?*
Où est-ce qu'on peut ...	Where can I/we ...	*oo es koñ puh ...*
... pêcher ?	... go fishing?	*... peh-shay ?*
... faire du cheval ?	... go riding?	*... fehr dew shuh-val ?*
Est-ce qu'il y a de bonnes plages (de sable) près d'ici ?	Are there any good (sandy) beaches near here?	*es keel ya duh bon plazh duh sabl preh dee-see ?*
Est-ce qu'il y a une piscine ?	Is there a swimming pool?	*es keel ya ewn pee-seen ?*
Aimes-tu ... ?	Do you like ...?	*em·tew ... ?*

Listen to Track 62

J'aime ...	I like ...	*zhem ...*
Je n'aime pas ...	I don't like ...	*zhe nem pa ...*

... l'art.	... art.	*... lar.*
... cuisiner.	... cooking.	*... kwee·zee·ney.*
... le cinema.	... movies.	*... le see·ney·ma.*
... les boîtes.	... nightclubs.	*... ley bwat.*
... lire.	... reading.	*... leer.*
... faire des courses.	... shopping.	*... fair dey koors.*
... le sport.	... sport.	*... le spor.*
... voyager.	... traveling.	*... vwa·ya·zhey.*
Aimes-tu ...	Do you like to ...	*em·tew ...*
... danser ?	... dance?	*... don·sey ?*
... aller aux concerts ?	... go to concerts?	*... a·ley o kon·sair ?*
... écouter de la musique ?	... listen to music?	*... ey·koo·tey de la mew·zeek ?*

Chapter 4.3: Music / la musique

Listen to Track 63

Je voudrais aller à un concert.	I would like to go to a concert.	*zhuh voo-dreh zallay ah uhn kaamsehr.*
Y-a-t-il de bons concerts en ce moment ?	Are there any good concerts on?	*eel ya duh boñ koñ-sehr ahñ suh momahñ ?*
Où est-ce qu'on peut avoir des billets pour le concert ?	Where can I get tickets for the concert?	*oo es koñ puh av-war day bee-yeh poor luh koñ-sehr ?*
Où est-ce qu'on peut aller écouter de la musique classique/du jazz ?	Where can we hear some classical music/jazz?	*oo es koñ puh a-lay ay-koo-tay duh la mew-zeek kla-seek/dew jaz ?*
Où pouvons-nous aller danser ?	Where can we go to dance?	*oo poo-vawn-noo al-lay dahnsay ?*
Dans une boîte de nuit.	To a night club.	*dahn zewn bwaht duh nwee.*
Voulez-vous danser ?	May I have this dance?	*voo-lay-voo dahn-say ?*

Listen to Track 64

Où sont les ...	Where can I find ...	*oo son ley ...*
... clubs ?	... clubs?	*... kleub ?*
... boîtes gay ?	... gay venues?	*... bwat gey ?*

... pubs, cafés ?	... pubs?	... *peub ?*
Je voudrais aller ...	I feel like going ...	*zhe voo·drey al-lay ...*
... à un concert.	... to a concert.	*... a ung kon·sair.*
... à la fête.	... to the party.	*... a la feyt.*

Chapter 4.4: Cinema / Le cinéma

Listen to Track 65

Je voudrais aller ...	I feel like going ...	*zhe voo·drey al-lay ...*
... au cinéma.	... to the movies.	*... o see·ney·ma.*
sous-titré	subtitled	*soo-tee-tray*
la séance	performance	*la sayahñs*
VO (version originale)	in the original language (i.e. not dubbed)	*vehr-syoñ o-ree-zhee-nal*
Qu'est-ce qui passe au cinéma?/ Qu'y-a-t-il comme films au cinema ?	What's on at the cinema?	*kes kee pas oh see-nay-ma ?*
Le film commence/ finit à quelle heure ?	When does the film start/finish?	*luh feelm ko-mahñs/fee-nee a kel ur ?*
C'est combien les billets?/ Combien coûtent les billets ?	How much are the tickets?	*say koñ-byañ lay bee-yeh ?*
Je voudrais deux places à euros.	I'd like two seats at ... euros.	*zhuh voo-dreh duh plas a ... uh-roh.*

Chapter 4.5: Theater and opera / Le théâtre et l'opéra

Listen to Track 66

Je voudrais aller ...	I feel like going ...	*zhe voo·drey al-lay ...*
... a l'opéra.	... to the opera.	*... ah loh-pay-ra.*
... au théâtre.	... to the theatre.	*... oh tay-ah-truh.*
la pièce (de théâtre)	play	*la pyes*
à l'orchestre	in the stalls	*a lor-kestr*
au balcon	in the circle	*oh bal-koñ*
le fauteuil	the seat	*luh foh-tuh-yuh*
le vestiaire	the cloakroom	*luh ves-tyehr*
l'entracte	the interval	*lahñ-trakt*
Qu'est-ce qu'on joue au théâtre/à l'opéra?	What is on at the theatre/at the opera?	*kes koñ zhoo oh tay-atr/a lo-pay-ra ?*
Les billets sont à combien ?	What prices are the tickets?	*lay bee-yeh soñ ta koñ-byañ ?*

Listen to Track 67

Je voudrais deux billets ...	I'd like two tickets ...	*zhuh voo-dreh duh bee-yeh ...*
... pour ce soir.	... for tonight.	*... poor suh swar.*
... pour demain soir.	... for tomorrow night.	*... poor duh-mañ swar.*
... pour le cinq août.	... for 5th August.	*... poor luh sañk oo(t).*

Quand est-ce que la représentation commence/ finit ?	When does the performance begin/end?	*kahñ tes kuh la ruh-pray-zahñ-ta-syoñ ko-mahñs/fee-nee ?*
Avez-vous des places pour ce soir ?	Do you have any seats for tonight?	*ah-vay voo day plass poor suh swahr ?*
Un fauteuil d'orchestre	an orchestra seat	*uhn foh-TUH-yuh dawr-kestruh*
une place réservée	*a reserved seat*	*ewn plas ray-zehr-vay*
au balcon	in the balcony	*oh bal-kawn*
la loge	the box	*la lawzh*
Pourrai-je bien voir de cet endroit ?	Can I see well from there?	*poo-ray zhuh byen vwahr duh set awndrwah ?*

Chapter 4.6: Television / La télévision

Listen to Track 68

la télécommande	the remote control	*la tay-lay-ko-mahñd*
le feuilleton	the soap	*luh fuh-yuh-toñ*
les informations	news	*lay zañ-for-ma-syoñ*
mettre en marche	to switch on	*metr ahñ marsh*
éteindre	to switch off	*ay-tañdr*
les dessins animés	cartoons	*lay deh-sañ a-nee-may*
Où est la television ?	Where is the television?	*oo ay la tay-lay-vee-zyoñ ?*
Comment la met-on en marche ?	How do you switch it on?	*ko-mahñ la meh toñ ahñ marsh ?*
Qu'est-ce qu'il y a à la télé ?	What is on television?	*kes keel ya a la tay-lay ?*
Les informations sont à quelle heure ?	When is the news?	*lay zañ-for-ma-syoñ soñ ta kel ur ?*
Est-ce qu'il y a des chaînes en anglais ?	Do you have any English-language channels?	*es keel ya day shen ahñ nahñ-gleh ?*
Avez-vous des vidéos en anglais ?	Do you have any English videos?	*a-vay voo day vee-day-o ahñ nahñ-gleh ?*

Chapter 4.7: Sports and exercise / Le sport et faire de l'exercice

Listen to Track 69

Où est-ce qu'on peut ...	Where can I/we ...	*oo es koñ puh ...*
... jouer au tennis ?	... play tennis?	*... zhoo-ay oh teh-nees ?*
... jouer au golf ?	... play golf?	*... zhoo-ay oh golf ?*
... faire de la natation ?	... go swimming?	*...fehr duh la na-ta-syoñ ?*
... faire du jogging ?	... go jogging?	*...fehr dew jo-geeng ?*
C'est combien l'heure ?	How much is it per hour?	*say koñ-byañ lur ?*
Est-ce qu'il faut être member ?	Do you have to be a member?	*es keel foh (t)etr mahñbr ?*
Est-ce qu'on peut louer ...	Can we hire (rent) ...	*es koñ puh loo-ay ...*
... des raquettes ?	... rackets?	*... day ra-ket ?*
... des clubs de golf ?	... golf clubs?	*... day club duh golf ?*
Nous voudrions aller voir jouer l'équipe de.	We'd like to go to see (name of team) play.	*noo voo-dryoñ a-lay vwar zhoo-ay laykeep duh.*
Où est-ce qu'on peut avoir des billets ?	Where can I/we get tickets?	*oo es koñ puh a-vwar day bee-yeh ?*

Qu'est-ce que vous faites comme sports ?	What sports do you play?	*kes kuh voo fet kom spor ?*
Il n'y a plus de billets pour le match.	There are no tickets left for the game.	*eel nya plew duh bee-yeh poor luh match.*

Chapter 4.8: Walking / Se promener

Listen to Track 70

Y a-t-il des promenades guides ?	Are there any guided walks?	*ee ya-teel day prom-nad gee-day ?*
Avez-vous un guide des promenades dans la region ?	Do you have a guide to local walks?	*a-vay vooz uñ geed day prom-nad dahñ la ray-zhyoñ ?*
Vous connaissez de bonnes promenades ?	Do you know any good walks?	*voo ko-neh-say duh bon prom-nad ?*
La promenade fait combien de kilomètres ?	How many kilometres is the walk?	*la prom-nad feh koñ-byañ duh kee-lo-metr ?*
Ça prendra combien de temps ?	How long will it take?	*sa prahñ-dra koñ-byañ duh tahñ ?*
Est-ce que ça monte dur ?	Is it very steep?	*es kuh sa moñt dewr ?*
Nous aimerions faire de l'escalade.	We'd like to go climbing.	*noo zeh-muh-ryoñ fehr duh les-ka-lad.*

Chapter 4.9: Telephone, mobile, and text messaging / Messagerie téléphonique, mobile et SMS (Textos)

Listen to Track 71

Je voudrais téléphoner.	I'd like to make a phone call.	*zhuh voo-dreh tay-lay-fo-nay.*
Il y a un télé-phone public ?	Is there a pay phone?	*eel ya uñ tay-lay-fon pew-bleek ?*
Une télécarte, s'il vous plaît ...	A phonecard, please ...	*ewn tay-lay-kart, seel voo pleh ...*
... de euros.	... for euros.	*... duh uh-roh.*
Vous avez un portable ?	Do you have a mobile?	*voo za-vay uñ por-tabl ?*
Quel est le numéro de votre portable ?	What's your mobile number?	*kel eh luh new-may-ro duh votr por-tabl ?*
Je peux emprunter votre portable ?	Can I use your mobile?	*zhuh puh ahñ-pruñ-tay votr por-tabl ?*
Le numéro de mon portable est le ...	My mobile number is ...	*luh new-may-ro duh moñ por-tabl ay luh ...*

Listen to Track 72

Âllo ?	Hello?	*Alo ?*
C'est de la part de qui ?	Who's calling?	*say duh la par duh kee ?*
De la part de ...	This is ...	*duh la par duh ...*
Un instant, s'il vous plait.	Just a moment.	*uñ nañ-stahñ seel voo pleh.*
Pourrais-je parler à ... ?	Can I speak to ...?	*poo-rezh par-lay a ... ?*

À l'appareil ...	It's (your name) ...	*a la-pa-ray ...*
Comment fait-on pour avoir une ligne extérieure ?	How do I get an outside line?	*ko-mahñ oñ feh poor a-vwar ewn leen-yuh ekstay-ree-ur ?*
Je vous rappellerai ...	I'll call back ...	*zhuh voo ra-pel-ray ...*
... plus tard.	... later.	*... plew tar.*
... demain.	... tomorrow.	*... duh-mañ.*
Je vous le/la passe.	I'm putting you through.	*zhuh voo luh/la pas.*
C'est occupé.	It's engaged (busy).	*say to-kew-pay.*

Listen to Track 73

Pouvez-vous rappeler plus tard ?	Can you call back later?	*poo-vay voo ra-play plew tar ?*
Voulez-vous laisser un message ?	Do you want to leave a message?	*voo-lay voo leh-say uñ meh-sazh ?*
Veuillez laisser votre message après le bip sonore.	Please leave a message after the tone.	*vuh-yay lay-say votr meh-sazh a-preh luh beep so-nor.*
S'il vous plaît, éteignez votre portable.	Please turn your mobile off.	*seel voo pleh, ay-ten-yay votr por-tabl.*
Je t'enverrai un message.	I will text you.	*zhuh tahñ-veh-ray uñ meh-sazh.*
Tu peux m'envoyer un message ?	Can you text me?	*tew puh mahñ-vwa-yay uñ meh-sazh ?*

Chapter 4.10: E-mail / Le courriel

Listen to Track 74

Nouveau message:	New message:	
A:	To:	
De:	From:	
Objet:	Subject:	
CC:	CC:	
Pièce jointe:	Attachment:	
Envoyer:	Send:	
Vous avez une adresse e-mail ?	Do you have an e-mail address?	*voo za-vay ewn a-dres ee-mehl ?*
Quelle est votre adresse e-mail ?	What's your e-mail address?	*kel ay votr a-dres ee-mehl ?*
Comment ça s'écrit ?	How do you spell it?	*ko-mahñ sa say-kree ?*
en un seul mot	all in one word	*ahñ uñ suhl moh*
tout en minuscules	all lower case	*too tahñ mee-new-skewl*
Mon adresse e-mail est ...	My e-mail address is ...	*moñ nad-res ee-mehl ay ...*
... xx.xx@ (nom de domaine). com/.fr/. co.uk	... xx.xx@ (company name).co.uk/com	*... xx pwañ xx a-roh-baz. pwañ say oh pwañ ew ka/. pwan come*
Je peux envoyer un e-mail ?	Can I send an e-mail?	*zhuh puh ahñ-vwa-yay uñ nee-mehl ?*
Est-ce que vous avez reçu mon e-mail ?	Did you get my e-mail?	*es-kuh voo za-vay ruh-sew moñ nee-mehl ?*

Chapter 4.11: Computer and internet / Ordinateur et internet

Listen to Track 75

accueil	home	*a-kuh-yuh*
nom d'utilisateur	username	*noñ dew-tee-lee-za-tur*
moteur de recherche	search engine	*mo-tur duh ruh-shehrsh*
mot de passe	password	*moh duh pas*
contactez-nous	contact us	*koñ-tak-tay-noo*
retour vers le sommaire	back to menu	*ruh-toor vehr luh som-mehr*
Est-ce qu'il y a des cybercafés par ici ?	Are there any internet cafés here?	*es keel ya day see-behr-ka-fay par eesee ?*
Combien coûte une heure de connexion ?	How much is it to log on for an hour?	*koñ-byañ koot ewn ur duh ko-neksyoñ ?*
Je n'arrive pas à me connecter.	I can't log on.	*zhuh na-reev pa a muh ko-nek-tay.*

Chapter 4.12: Fax

Listen to Track 76

À/De :	To/From:	
Objet :	Re:	
nombre de pages	number of pages	
Veuillez trouver ci-joint ...	Please find attached ...	
Avez-vous un fax ?	Do you have a fax?	*a-vay voo uñ fax ?*
Je voudrais envoyer un fax.	I want to send a fax.	*zhuh voo-dreh ahñ-vwa-yay uñ fax.*
Quel est votre numéro de fax ?	What is your fax number?	*kel ay votr new-may-roh duh fax ?*
Mon numéro de fax est le ...	My fax number is ...	*moñ new-may-roh duh fax ay luh ...*

Chapter 5: Talking about mealtimes and eating / Parler de l'heure des repas et de l'alimentation

One of the best ways to enjoy life is to indulge in food and drink. It is a happy occurrence when you are able to do this while learning a language. Once you have learned some basic French vocabulary and phrases related to eating and drinking, you can reward yourself with a trip to a French restaurant or café to put these skills to good use. Even better, if you get the chance to go to a French speaking country, you will find that this vocabulary comes in very handy.

Chapter 5.1: At the restaurant / Au restaurant

Listen to Track 77

un restaurant	a restaurant	*un res-to-ron*
Où peut-on trouver un bon restaurant ?	Where is there a good restaurant?	*oo puh-tawn troo-vay uhn bawn ress-taw-rawn ?*
Je voudrais réserver une table pour ... personnes ...	I'd like to book a table for ... people ...	*zhuh voo-dreh ray-zehr-vay ewn tabl poor ... pehr-son ...*
... pour ce soir / pour demain soir / pour dix-neuf heures trente.	... for tonight / for tomorrow night / for 7.30.	*... poor suh swar / poor duh-mañ swar / poor deez-nuh vur trahñt.*
Je voudrais ..., s'il vous plaît.	I'd like ..., please.	*zhe voo-drey ..., seel voo pley.*

... une table pour (cinq) personnes,	... a table for (five),	... ewn ta-ble poor (sungk) pair-son,
...une table pour deux,	...a table for two,	...ewn tabl poor duh,
... un endroit pour (non-) fumeurs,	... the (non-) smoking section,	... un on-drwa poor non-few-muhr,
Le menu, s'il vous plaît.	The menu, please.	luh muh-new, seel voo pleh.
Je prendrai le menu à euros, s'il vous plaît.	I'll have the menu at euros, please.	zhuh prahñ luh muh-new a uh-roh, seel voo pleh.

Listen to Track 78

Reading the menu:

Plat du jour à €7.50 – poisson ou viande ou volaille garnis
Dish of the day €7.50 – fish or meat or poultry with veg and French fries

Menu du midi – entrée + plat + café
Lunchtime menu – starter + main course + coffee

Qu'est-ce que vous prenez ?	What will you have?	kes kuh voo pruh-nay ?
Qu'est-ce que vous conseillez ?	What would you recommend?	kes-ke voo kon-sey-yey ?
Pouvez-vous nous recommander un plat regional ?	Can you recommend a local dish?	poo-vay voo noo ruh-ko-mahñ-day uñ pla ray-zhyo-nal ?

Quelle est la spécialité locale ?	What's the local speciality?	*kel ey la spey-sya-lee-tey lo-kal ?*
Quel est le plat du jour ?	What is the dish of the day?	*kel eh luh pla dew zhoor ?*
Qu'est-ce qu'il y a dedans ?	What is in this?	*kes keel ya duh-dahñ ?*
Je prends ça.	I'll have this.	*zhuh prahñ sa.*
Encore du pain ...	More bread ...	*ahñ-kor dew pañ ...*
Encore de l'eau ...	More water ...	*ahñ-kor duh loh ...*

Listen to Track 79

... s'il vous plaît.	... please.	*... seel voo pleh*
l'addition	the bill	*la-dee-syon*
la carte des boissons	the drink list	*la kart dey bwa-son*
la carte	the menu	*la kart*
ce plat	that dish	*suh pla*
la carte des vins	the wine list	*la kart dey vun*
le petit déjeuner	breakfast	*luh puh-tee day-zhuh-nay*
le déjeuner	lunch	*luh day-zhuh-nay*
le dîner	dinner	*luh dee-nay*
le souper	supper	*luh soo-pay*
un sandwich	a sandwich	*uhn sahnd-weetsh*
un casse-croûte	a snack	*uhn kass-kroot*

Listen to Track 80

À quelle heure servez-vous le dîner ?	At what time is dinner served?	*ah keh luhr sehr-vay-voo luh dee-nay ?*
Pouvons-nous déjeuner (dîner) maintenant ?	Can we have lunch (dinner) now?	*poo-vaum-noo day-zhuh-nay (dee-nay) ment-nahn ?*
la serveuse	the waitress	*la sehr-vuhz*
le garçon	the waiter	*luh gar-saum*
le maître d'hôtel	the headwaiter	*luh meh-truh doh-tel*
Garçon !	Waiter!	*garsawn !*
Nous sommes deux.	There are two of us.	*noo sawm duh.*
Donnez-moi une table près de la fenêtre.	Give me a table near the window.	*daw-nay-mwah ewn TA-bluh preh duh la fuh-NEH-truh.*
Nous voulons dîner à la carte.	We want to dine à la carte.	*noo voo-lawn dee-nay ah la kart.*
à prix fixe	table	*ah pree feeks*
Servez-nous vite, s'il vous plaît.	Please serve us quickly.	*sehr-vay-noo veet, seel voo pleh.*
Apportez-moi le menu.	Bring me the menu.	*ap-pawr-tay-mwah luh muh-new.*

Listen to Track 81

une fourchette	a fork	*ewn foor-shet*

un couteau	a knife	*uhn koo-toh*
une assiette	a plate	*ewn as-syet*
une cuillère à café	a teaspoon	*ewn kwee-yeh rah ka-fay*
une cuillère à soupe	a tablespoon	*ewn kwee-yeh rah soop*
la tasse	cup	*lah tass*
Je désire quelque chose de simple.	I want something simple.	*zhuh day-zeer kel-kuh shohz duh SEN-pluh.*
Pas trop épicé.	Not too spicy.	*pah troh pay-pee-say.*
J'aime la viande saignante.	I like the meat rare.	*zhem la vee-ahnd sayn-yahnt.*
Bien cuite.	Well done.	*byen kweet.*
Emportez cela, s'il vous plaît.	Take it away, please.	*ahn-pawr-tay suh-la, seel voo pleh.*
C'est froid.	This is cold.	*Seh frwah.*
Je n'ai pas commandé cela.	I did not order this.	*zhuh nay pah kaw-mahn-day suh-la.*
Pouvez-vous remplacer cela par une salade ?	May I change this for a salad?	*poo-vay-voo rahn-plasay suh-la par ewn sa-lad ?*

Listen to Track 82

l'eau potable	drinking water	*loh paw-ta-bluh*
avec de la glace / sans glace	with ice / without ice	*a-vek duh la glas / sahn glas*
le dessert	dessert	*luh desair*

le poisson	fish	*luh pwasson*
le verre	glass	*luh vair*
le plat principal	main course	*luh pla pranseepal*
le poivre	pepper	*luh pwahvr*
le salade	salad	*luh sa-lad*
le sel	salt	*luh cell*
le potage	soup	*luh potahj*
la cuillère	spoon	*la kwee-yair*
l'entrée	starter/ appetizer	*lontray*

Listen to Track 83

Encore ..., s'il vous plaît.	Another ..., please.	*onkor ..., seel voo play.*
L'addition, s'il vous plaît.	The check, please.	*la-dee-syawn, seel voo pleh.*
L'addition, s'il vous plaît !	The bill, please!	*ladeess-yon seel voo play !*
Le pourboire est-il compris ?	Is the tip included?	*luh poor-bwahr eh-teel kawn-pree ?*
Le service est-il compris ?	Is the service charge included?	*luh sehr-veess eh-teel kawn-pree ?*
Il y a une erreur dans l'addition.	There is a mistake in the bill.	*eelya ewn ehr-ruhr dahn la-dee-syawn.*
Pourquoi ces supplements ?	What are these charges for?	*poor-kwah say sew-play-mahn ?*
Gardez la monnaie.	Keep the change.	*gar-day la maw-neh.*
La cuisine et le service étaient excellents.	The food and service were excellent.	*la kwee-zeen ay luh sehr-veess ay-teh tex-eh-lahn.*

Chapter 5.2: Foods / Les aliments

Listen to Track 84

le pain	bread	*luh pehn*
le beurre	butter	*luh buhr*
le sucre	sugar	*luh sew-kruh*
le sel	salt	*luh sel*
le poivre	pepper	*luh pwah-vruh*
la sauce	sauce	*la sohss*
l'huile	oil	*iweel*
le vinaigre	vinegar	*luh vee-neh-gruh*
la moutarde	mustard	*la moo-tard*
l'ail	garlic	*lahyuh*

Listen to Track 85

du poulet rôti	roast chicken	*dew poo-leh roh-tee*
du poulet frit	fried chicken	*dew poo-leh free*
du boeuf	beef	*dew buhf*
du canard	duck	*dew ka-nar*
de l'oie	goose	*duh iwah*
du gigot	lamb	*dew zhee-goh*
du foie	liver	*dew fwah*
du homard	lobster	*dew aw-mar*
du porc	pork	*dew pawr*
du rosbif	roast beef	*dew raws-beef*
des sardines	sardines	*day sar-deen*
du bifteck	steak	*dew bif-tek*
des crevettes	shrimps	*day kruh-vet*
de la saucisse	sausage	*duh la saw-sees*
du veau	veal	*dew voh*

Listen to Track 86

baba au rhum	small sponge cake, often with raisins, soaked in a rum-flavoured syrup	*ba-ba o rom*
béarnaise (f)	white sauce of wine or vinegar beaten with egg yolks & flavoured with herbs	*bey-ar-neyz*
blanquette de veau (f)	veal stew in white sauce with cream	*blong-ket de vo*
bombe glacée (f)	ice cream with candied fruits, glazed chestnuts & cream	*bom-be gla-sey*
bouillabaisse (f)	fish soup stewed in a broth with garlic, orange peel, fennel, tomatoes & saffron	*bwee-ya-bes*
brioche (f)	small roll or cake sometimes flavoured with nuts, currants or candied fruits	*bree-yosh*
brochette (f)	grilled skewer of meat or vegetables	*bro-shet*
consommé (m)	clarified meat or fish-based broth	*kon-so-mey*
contre-filet (m)	beef sirloin roast	*kon-tre-fee-ley*

coulis (m)	fruit or vegetable purée, used as a sauce	*koo-lee*
croque-madame (m)	grilled or fried ham & cheese sandwich, topped with a fried egg	*krok-ma-dam*
croquembouche (m)	cream puffs dipped in caramel	*kro-kom-boosh*
croque-monsieur (m)	grilled or fried ham & cheese sandwich	*krok-mes-yeu*

Listen to Track 87

croustade (f)	puff pastry filled with fish, seafood, meat, mushrooms, or vegetables	*kroo-stad*
dijonnaise	dishes with a mustard-based sauce	*dee-zho-nez*
estouffade (f)	meat stewed in wine with carrots & herbs	*es-too-fad*
friand (m)	pastry stuffed with minced sausage meat, ham & cheese, or almond cream	*free-yon*
fricandeau (m)	veal fillet simmered in white wine, vegetables herbs & spices / a pork pâté	*free-kon-do*

fricassée (f)	lamb, veal or poultry in a thick creamy sauce with mushrooms & onions	*free-ka-sey*
grenadin (m)	veal (or sometimes poultry) fillet, wrapped in a thin slice of bacon	*gre-na-dun*
michette (f)	savoury bread stuffed with cheese, olives, onions & anchovies	*mee-shet*
pain-bagnat (m)	small round bread loaves, filled with onions, vegetables, anchovies & olives	*pun ban-ya*
plateau de fromage (m)	cheese board or platter	*pla-to de fro-mazh*
pomme duchesse (f)	fritter of mashed potato, butter & egg yolk	*pom dew-shes*
pot-au-feu (m)	beef, root vegetable & herb stockpot	*po-to-fe*
potée (f)	meat & vegetables cooked in a pot	*po-tey*
profiterole (m)	small pastry with savoury or sweet fillings	*pro-fee-trol*
puits d'amour (m)	puff pastry filled with custard or jam	*pwee da-moor*

Listen to Track 88

quenelle (f)	fish or meat dumpling, often poached	*ke-nel*
quiche (f)	tart with meat, fish, or vegetable filling	*keesh*
raclette (f)	hot melted cheese, served with potatoes & gherkins	*ra-klet*
ragoût (m)	stew of meat, fish and/or vegetables	*ra-goo*
ratatouille (f)	vegetable stew	*ra-ta-too-ye*
roulade (f)	slice of meat or fish rolled around stuffing	*roo-lad*
savarin (m)	sponge cake soaked with a rum syrup & filled with custard, cream & fruits	*sa-va-run*
savoie (f)	light cake made with beaten egg whites	*sav-wa*
tartiflette (f)	dish of potatoes, cheese & bacon	*tar-tee-flet*
velouté (m)	rich, creamy soup, usually prepared with vegetables, shellfish or fish purée	*vew-loo-tay*

vol-au-vent (m)	puff pastry filled with a mixture of sauce & meat, seafood or vegetables	*vo-lo-von*
Je voudrais du potage au poulet.	I want some chicken soup.	*zhuh day-zeer dew paw-tazh oh poo-leh.*
du potage aux légumes	some vegetable soup	*dew paw-tazh oh lay-gewm*

Chapter 5.3: Breakfast foods / Le petit-déjeuner

Listen to Track 89

Puis-je avoir du jus de fruit ?	May I have some fruit juice?	*PWEE-zhuh a-vwahr dew zhew duhfrwee ?*
du jus d'orange	orange juice	*dew zhew daw-rahnzh*
des pruneaux cuits	stewed prunes	*day prew-noh kwee*
du jus de tomate	tomato juice	*dew zhew duh taw-maht*
des toasts avec de la confiture	toast and jam	*day tohst a-vek duh la kawn-fet-tewr*
des petits pains	rolls	*day puh-tee pen*
une omelette	an omelet	*ewn awm-let*
des œufs à la coque	soft-boiled eggs	*day zuh ah la kawk*
des œufs quatre minutes	medium-boiled eggs	*day zhuh ka-truh mee-newt*
des œufs durs	hard-boiled eggs	*day zuh dewr*
des œufs sur le plat	fried eggs	*day zuh sewr luh pla*
des œufs brouillés	scrambled eggs	*day zuh broo-yay*
des œufs avec du lard	bacon and eggs	*day zuh a-vek dew lar*
des œufs au jambon	ham and eggs	*day zuh oh zhawn-bawn*

Chapter 5.4: Special diets & allergies / Les régimes spéciaux et les allergies alimentaires

Listen to Track 90

Y a-t-il un restaurant végétarien par ici ?	Is there a vegetarian restaurant near here?	*ya-teel un res-to-ron vey-zhey-ta-ryun par ee-see ?*
Est-ce qu'il y a des restaurants végétariens ici ?	Are there any vegetarian restaurants here?	*es keel ya day res-toh-rahñ vay-zhay-ta-ryañ ee-see ?*
Vous faites des repas végétariens ?	Do you have vegetarian food?	*voo fet ley re-pa vey-zhey-ta-ryun ?*
Vous avez des plats végétariens ?	Do you have any vegetarian dishes?	*voo za-vay day pla vay-zhay-ta-ryañ ?*
Quels sont les plats sans viande/poisson ?	Which dishes have no meat/fish?	*kel soñ lay plah sahñ vyahñd/pwasoñ ?*
Pouvez-vous préparer un repas sans ...	Could you prepare a meal without ...	*poo-vey-voo prey-pa-rey un re-pa son ...*
... beurre ?	... butter?	*... beur ?*
... œufs ?	... eggs?	*... zeu ?*
... bouillon gras ?	... meat stock?	*... boo-yon gra ?*

Listen to Track 91

Je suis allergique ...	I'm allergic ...	*zhe swee za-lair-zheek ...*
... aux produits laitiers.	... to dairy produce.	*... o pro-dwee ley-tyey.*
... au gluten.	... to gluten.	*... o glew-ten.*
... au glutamate de sodium.	... to MSG.	*... o glew-ta-mat de so-dyom.*
... au noix.	... to nuts.	*... oh nwa.*
... aux fruits de mer.	... to seafood.	*... oh frwee de mair.*
Je voudrais des pâtes comme plat principal.	I'd like pasta as a main course.	*zhuh voo-dreh day pat kom pla prañ-see-pal.*
Je n'aime pas la viande.	I don't like meat.	*zhuh nehm pa la vyahñd.*
Est-ce que c'est fait avec du bouillon de legumes ?	Is it made with vegetable stock?	*es kuh say feh a-vek dew boo-yoñ duh lay-gewm ?*

Chapter 5.5: Vegetables and salad / Légumes et salades

Listen to Track 92

Je voudrais des asperges.	I want some asparagus.	*zhuh day-zeer day zas-pehrzh.*
des carottes	carrots	*day ka-rawt*
du chou	cabbage	*dew shoo*
des haricots	beans	*day a-ri-koh*
du chou-fleur	cauliflower	*dew shoo-fluhr*
du céleri et des olives	celery and olives	*dew sayl-ree ay day zaw-leev*
du concombre	cucumber	*dew kawn-kawn-bruh*
de la laitue	lettuce	*duh la leh-tew*
des champignons	mushrooms	*day shahn-peen-yawn*

Listen to Track 93

des oignons	onions	*day zawn-yawn*
des petits pois	peas	*day puh-tee pwah*
des poivrons	peppers	*day pwahv-rawn*
des pommes de terre bouillies	boiled potatoes	*day pawm duh tehr boo-yee*
des pommes de terre frites	fried potatoes	*day pawm duh tehr freet*
de la purée de pommes de terre	mashed potatoes	*duh la pew-ray duh pawm duh tehr*
du riz	rice	*dew ree*
des épinards	spinach	*day zay-pee-nahr*
des tomates	tomatoes	*day taw-maht*

Chapter 5.6: Fruits / Les fruits

Listen to Track 94

Je voudrais une pomme.	I want an apple.	*zhuh day-zee rewn pawm.*
des cerises	cherries	*day suh-reez*
un pamplemousse	a grapefruit	*ewn pahn-pluh-mooss*
du raisin	grapes	*dew ray-zen*
du citron	lemon	*dew see trawn*
du melon	melon	*dew muh-lawn*
des noix	nuts	*day nwah*
une orange	an orange	*ew naw-rahnzh*
une pêche	a peach	*ewn pesh*
des framboises	raspberries	*day frahn-bwahz*
des fraises	strawberries	*day frayz*

Chapter 5.7: Desserts / Les desserts

Listen to Track 95

Puis-je avoir du gâteau ?	May I have some cake?	*Pwee-zhah-vwahr dew gah-toh ?*
du fromage	cheese	*dewfraw-mazh*
des petits gâteaux (secs)	cookies	*duh puh-tee gah-toh sek*
des crêpes suzette	crêpes suzette	*day krep sew-zet*
de la crème renversée	custard cream	*duh la krem rahn-vehr-say*
de la glace au chocolat	chocolate ice cream	*duh la glas oh shaw-kaw-la*
de la glace à la vanille	vanilla ice cream	*duh la glas ah la va-nee-yuh*

Chapter 5.8: Beverages & drinks / Les boissons

Listen to Track 96

l'eau minérale f	mineral water	*lo meenayral*
une bouteille d'eau minérale	a bottle of mineral water	*ewn boo-tay doh mee-nay-ral*
un jus de fruit	a fruit drink	*uhn zhew duhfrwee*
le jus d'orange	orange juice	*luh joo doronj*
une boisson gazeuse	a soda	*ewn bwahsawn ga-zuhz*
la boisson non-alcoolisée	a soft drink	*la bwasson non-alkoleezay*
l'eau	water	*lo*
une orangeade	an orangeade	*ewn o-rahñ-zhad*
au citron	with lemon	*oh see-troñ*
de l'eau minérale	some mineral water	*duh loh mee-nay-ral*
du lait	milk	*dew leh*
du thé	tea	*dew tay*
de la citronnade	lemonade	*duh la see-traw-nad*
gazeuse	sparkling	*ga-zuhz*

Listen to Track 97

plate	still	*plat*
citron pressé	fresh lemon juice	*seetron pressay*
diabolo menthe/fraise	mint/strawberry (cordial with lemonade)	*d-yabolo mont/ frez*

eau minérale gazeuse	sparkling mineral water	*o meenayral gazurz*
infusion	herb tea	*anfooz-yon*
jus	juice	*joo*
jus de pommes	apple juice	*joo duh pom*
lait fraise/ grenadine	milk with strawberry/ grenadine cordial	*lay frez/ gruhnadeen*
marc	clear spirit distilled from grape pulp	*mar*
menthe à l'eau	mint cordial	*mont a lo*
orange pressée	fresh orange juice	*oronj pressay*

Listen to Track 98

thé à la menthe	mint tea	*tay ah la mont*
thé au lait	tea with milk	*tay o lay*
thé citron	lemon tea	*tay seetron*
thé nature	tea without milk	*tay natoor*
tilleul	lime-flower tea	*tee-yurl*
thé à la verveine	verbena tea	*tay ah la vairven*
minérale non-gazeuse	still mineral	*mee-ney-ral nong-ga-zeuz*

Chapter 5.9: In a café / dans un café

Listen to Track 99

un café	a café	*ung ka-fey*
du café noir	black coffee	*dew ka-fay nwahr*
un café crème	coffee with cream	*uhn ka-fay kraym*
un (café) crème	white creamy coffee	*uñ (ka-fay) krem*
un grand crème	large white creamy coffee	*uñ grahñ krem*
un café au lait	coffee with hot milk	*uñ ka-fay oh leh*
un café	a coffee	*uñ ka-fay*
le sucre	sugar	*luh sookr*
sans sucre	no sugar	*sahñ sewkr*
pour deux personnes	for two	*poor duh pehr-son*
pour moi	for me	*poor mwa*
pour lui/elle	for him/her	*poor lwee/el*
pour nous	for us	*poor noo*

Listen to Track 100

avec des glaçons, s'il vous plaît	with ice, please	*a-vek day gla-soñ, seel voo pleh*
café glacé	iced coffee	*kafay glassay*
café soluble	instant coffee	*kafay soloobl*
café viennois	coffee with whipped cream	*kafay vee-enwa*

thé à la camomille	chamomile tea	*tay ah la kamomee*
capiteux	heady	*kapeetuh*
chambré	at room temperature	*shonbray*
chocolat chaud	hot chocolate	*shokola sho*
chocolat glacé	iced chocolate drink	*shokola glassay*
décaféiné	decaffeinated	*daykafay-eenay*
frappé	blended ice	*frapay*
(un) café	(cup of) coffee	*(ung) ka-fey*
(un) thé	(cup of) tea	*(un) tey*
au lait	with milk	*o ley*
sans sucre	without sugar	*son sew-kre*
chaude	hot	*shod*

Chapter 5.10: Bar, wines, and spirits / Bar, vins et spiritueux

Listen to Track 101

un bar	a bar	*um bar*
le barman	the bartender	*luh bar-mahn*
une boisson	a drink	*ewn bwahsawn*
digestif	liqueur	*deejesteef*
La carte des vins, s'il vous plaît.	The wine list, please.	*la kart day vañ, seel voo pleh.*
du vin blanc/ du vin rouge	white wine/red wine	*dew vañ blahñ/ dew vañ roozh*
Pouvez-vous nous recommander un bon vin?	Can you recommend a good wine?	*poo-vay voo noo ruh-ko-mahñ-day uñ boñ vañ?*
Une bouteille ...	A bottle ...	*ewn boo-tay-yuh ...*
Un pichet ...	A carafe ...	*uñ pee-sheh ...*
... de la cuvée du patron.	... of the house wine.	*... duh la kew-vay dew pa-troñ.*
Qu'est-ce que vous avez comme digestifs?	What liqueurs do you have?	*Kes kuh voo za-vay kom dee-zheh-steef?*

Listen to Track 102

Je prendrai ...	I'll have ...	*zhe pron ...*
la bière	beer	*la bee-air*
le gin	gin	*luh djeen*

le porto	port	*luh portoh*
le vin rouge	red wine	*luh van rooj*
le rosé	rosé	*luh rozzay*
le vin blanc	white wine	*luh van blon*
le vin	wine	*luh van*
la carte des vins	wine list	*la kart day van*
alcool	alcohol	*alkool*

Listen to Track 103

Bière (à la) pression	draught beer	*bee-air press-yon*
Bière brune	bitter; dark beer	*bee-air broon*
Bière rousse	relatively sweet, fairly dark beer	*bee-air rooss*
Blanc de blancs	white wine from white grapes	*blon duh blon*
Blanquette de Limoux	sparkling white wine from Languedoc	*blonket duh leemoo*
Bourgogne	wine from the Burgundy area	*boor-goh-nyuh*
Brouilly	red wine from the Beaujolais area	*broo-yee*
Brut	very dry	*brOOt*
Champagne	champagne	*Shonpah-nyuh*
Champagnisé	sparkling	*shonpan-yeezay*
Chartreuse	herb liqueur	*shartrurz*
Château-Margaux	red wine from the Bordeaux area	*shato margo*
Châteauneuf-du-Pape	red wine from the Rhône valley	*shatonurf doo pap*

Listen to Track 104

Cidre	cider	*seedr*
Cidre bouché	cider in bottle with a cork	*seedr booshay*
Cidre doux	sweet cider	*seedr doo*
51® (cinquante-et-un)	a brand of pastis	*sankontay-an*
Cognac	brandy	*konyak*
Crème de cassis	blackcurrant liqueur	*krem duh kasseess*
Cru	vintage	*kroo*
Demi	small draught beer; quarter of a litre of beer	*duhmee*
Demi-sec	medium dry	*duhmee-sek*
Eau de vie	spirit made from fruit	*o duh vee*
Fendant	Swiss dry white wine	*fondon*
Fine	fine brandy, liqueur brandy	*feen*
Fleurie	red wine from Beaujolais	*flurree*
Gazeux	fizzy	*gazur*
Gewurztraminer	dry white wine from Alsace	*guh-woorztrameenair*

Listen to Track 105

Glaçon	ice cube	*glasson*
Grand cru	fine vintage	*gron kroo*

Graves	red wine from the Bordeaux area	*Grahv*
Médoc	red wine from the Bordeaux area	*Maydok*
Meursault	wine from Burgundy	*murrso*
Muscadet	dry white wine from the Nantes area	*mooskaday*
Muscat	sweet white wine	*mooska*
Noilly-Prat	an aperitif wine similar to Dry Martini	*nwa-yee pra*
Nuits-Saint-Georges	red wine from Burgundy	*nwee San jorj*
Panaché	shandy	*panashay*
Passe-Tout-Grain	red wine from Burgundy	*pass too gran*
Pastis	aniseed-flavoured alcoholic drink	*pasteess*
Pernod	a brand of pastis	*Pairno*
Pouilly-Fuissé	dry white wine from Burgundy	*poo-yee-fweessay*
Premier cru	vintage wine	*pruhm-yay croo*

Listen to Track 106

Pression	draught beer, draught	*press-yon*
Rhum	rum	*rom*
Ricard	a brand of pastis	*reekar*
Rosé	rosé wine	*rozzay*

Rouge	red	*rooj*
Saint-Amour	red wine from Beaujolais	*santamoor*
Saint-Emilion	red wine from the Bordeaux area	*san-taymeelee-yon*
Sauternes	fruity white wine from the Bordeaux area	*sotairn*
Sec	dry; neat	*sek*
Sirop	cordial	*seero*
Vin de pays	regional wine	*Van duh payee*
Vin de table	table wine	*Van duh tahbl*
Vin rosé	rosé wine	*Van rozzay*
Yvorne	Swiss dry white wine	*eevorn*

Listen to Track 107

Je vous offre un verre.	I'll buy you a drink.	*zhe voo zo-fre un vair*
Qu'est-ce que vous voulez ?	What would you like?	*kes-ke voo voo-ley ?*
Santé !	Cheers!	*son-tey !*
cocktail m	cocktail	*kok-tel*
un petit verre de (whisky)	a shot of (whisky)	*um pe-tee vair de (wees-kee)*
une bouteille de vin	a bottle of wine	*ewn boo-tey de vun*
un verre de vin	a glass of wine	*un vair de vun*
une bouteille	a bottle	*ewn boo-tey*

Chapter 6: Safe travel and planning / Voyager en toute sécurité et planification

Learning French often inspires you to daydream about traveling and planning trips to French-speaking countries. This type of wanderlust can be greatly expedited with some French vocabulary and phrases related to traveling and planning. From the beach to the mountains, from camping to sightseeing, this chapter will give you some practical and useful hints for planning your dream holiday.

Chapter 6.1: Accomodation / Hébergements

Listen to Track 108

Je cherche un bon hôtel.	I am looking for a good hotel.	*zhuh shehrsh uhn baw noh-tel.*
... un hôtel à prix modéré.	... an inexpensive hotel.	*... uh noh-tel ah pree maw-day-ray.*
... une pension.	... a boarding house.	*... ewn pahnsyaum.*
... un appartement meuble.	... full furnished apartment.	*... uh nap-par-tuh-mahn muh-blay.*
Je (ne) veux (pas) être au centre ville.	I (do not) want to be at the center of town.	*zhuh (nuh) vuh (pah) eytruh oh sen-truh veal.*
Où il n'y a pas de bruit.	Where it is not noisy.	*oo eel nee a pah duh brwee.*
J'ai réservé une chambre pour aujourd'hui.	I have a reservation for today.	*zhay ray-zehr-vay ewn SHAHNbruh poor oh-zhoord-wee.*

Avez-vous une chambre disponible ?	Do you have a room/a vacancy?	*a-vay-voo zewn SHAHNbruh ?*
une chambre climatisée	an air-conditioned room	*ewn shahn-bruh klee-ma-teezay*
une chambre à un lit	a single room	*ewn shahn-bruh ah uhn lee*
une chambre pour deux personnes	a double room	*ewn shahnbruh poor duh pehrsaum*

Listen to Track 109

avec repas	with meals	*a-vek ruh-pah*
sans repas	without meals	*sahn ruh-pah*
avec un grand lit	with a double bed	*uhn grahn lee*
avec salle de bain	with a bathroom	*a-vek sol duh ben*
avec une douche	*with a shower*	*a-vek ewn doosh*
avec lits jumeaux	with twin beds	*a-vek lee zhew-moh*
un appartement	a suite	*uh nap-par-tuh-mahn*
pour cette nuit	for tonight	*poor set nwee*
pour trois jours	for three days	*poor trwah zhoor*
pour deux personnes	for two	*poor duh pehrsawn*

Listen to Track 110

Quel est le coût par jour ?	What is the rate per day?	*keh leh VAW truh pree par zhoor ?*
Est-ce que les taxes et le service sont compris ?	Are tax and room service included?	*ess-kuh lay tax ay luh serveess sawn kawn-pree ?*
Je voudrais bien voir la chambre.	I would like to see the room.	*zhuh voodreh byen vwahr la SHAHN-bruh.*
Je n'aime pas celle-ci.	I do not like this one.	*zhuh nem pah sel-see.*
en haut	upstairs	*ahn oh*
en bas	downstairs	*ahn bah*
Y a-t-il un ascenseur ?	Is there an elevator?	*ee a-tee luh nasawnsuhr ?*
Le service, s'il vous plaît.	Room service, please.	*luh sehr-veess, seel voo pleh.*
Faites monter un porteur dans ma chambre, s'il vous plaît.	Please send a porter to my room.	*fet mawn-tay uhn pawrtuhr dahn ma SHAHNbruh, seel voo pleh.*
une femme de chambre	a chambermaid	*ewn fahm duh shahn-bruh*
un chasseur	a bellhop	*uhn shas-suhr*

Listen to Track 111

Veuillez m'appeler à neuf heures.	Please call me at nine o'clock.	*vuh-yay map-lay ah nuh vuhr.*

Je désire avoir le petit déjeuner dans ma chambre.	I want breakfast in my room.	*zhuh day-zeer avwahr luh puh-tee day-zhuhnay dahn ma SHAHN-bruh.*
Revenez plus tard.	Come back later.	*ruh-vuh-nay plew tar.*
Apportez-moi encore une couverture.	Bring me another blanket.	*ap-pawr-tay-mwah ahnkawr ewn koo-vair-tewr.*
un oreiller	a pillow	*uh naw-ray-yay*
une taie d'oreiller	a pillowcase	*ewn tay daw-ray-yay*
des cintres	hangers	*day sanhg-truh*
le savon	soap	*luh sa-vawn*
les serviettes	towels	*lay sehr-vee-et*
un tapis de bain	a bath mat	*uhn ta-pee duh ben*
la baignoire	the bathtub	*la ben-wahr*
le lavabo	the sink	*luh la-va-boh*
le papier hygiénique	toilet paper	*luh pap-yay ee zhay neek*

Listen to Track 112

Je voudrais parler au gérant.	I would like to speak to the manager.	*zhuh voo-dreh parlay oh zhay-rahn.*
Ma clé, s'il vous plaît !	My room key, please!	*ma klay, seel voo pleh !*
Y a-t-il des lettres ou des messages pour moi ?	Do I have any letters or messages?	*ee a-teel day leh-truh oo day messazh poor mwah ?*

Quel est le numéro de ma chambre ?	What is my room number?	*keh leh luh new-mayroh duh ma SHAHN-bruh ?*
Je pars à dix heures.	I am leaving at ten o'clock.	*zhuh par ah dee zuhr.*
Veuillez préparer ma note.	Please make out my bill.	*vuh-yay pray-pa-ray ma nawt.*
Acceptez-vous les cheques ?	Will you accept a check?	*voo-lay-voo byen akseptay uhn chayck ?*
Veuillez faire suivre mon courrier à ...	Please forward my mail to ...	*vuh-yay fehr SWEEvruh mawn koor-yay ah ...*
Puis-je vous laisser des bagages jusqu'à demain ?	May I store baggage here until tomorrow?	*PWEE-zhuh voo lessay day bagazh zhews-kah duh-man ?*

Listen to Track 113

Où est-ce qu'on peut trouver	Where's a ...	*oo es·kon peu troo·vey*
... un terrain de camping ?	... camping ground?	*... un tey·run de kom·peeng ?*
... une pension ?	... guesthouse?	*... ewn pon·see·on ?*
... un hôtel ?	... hotel?	*... un o·tel ?*
... une auberge de jeunesse ?	... youth hostel?	*... ewn o·bairzh de zhe·nes ?*

Est-ce que vous pouvez recommander un logement ...	Can you recommend somewhere...	es·ke voo poo·vey re·ko·mon·dey un lozh·mon ...
... pas cher ?	... cheap?	... pa shair ?
... de bonne qualité ?	... good?	... de bon ka·lee·tey ?
... près d'ici ?	... nearby?	... prey dee·see ?
Je voudrais réserver une chambre, s'il vous plaît.	I'd like to book a room, please.	zhe voo·drey rey·zair·vey ewn shom·bre seel voo pley
J'ai une réservation.	I have a reservation.	zhey ewn rey·zair·va·syon
Mon nom est ...	My name is ...	mon nom ey ...

Listen to Track 114

Avez-vous une ... chambre ?	Do you have a ... room?	a·vey·voo ewn ... shom·bre ?
... à un lit ...	... single ...	... a un lee ...
... avec un grand lit ...	... double ...	... a·vek ung gron lee ...
... des lits jumeaux ...	... twin ...	... dey lee zhew·mo ...
Est-ce qu' on peut payer avec ...	Can I pay by ...	es·kom peu pey·yey a·vek ...
... une carte de crédit ?	... credit card?	... ewn kart de krey·dee ?
... des chèques de voyage ?	... travelers cheque?	... dey shek de vwa·yazh ?
Quel est le prix par ...	How much is it per ...	kel ey le pree par ...

... nuit ?	... night?	...nwee ?
... personne ?	... person?	... pair·son ?

Listen to Track 115

Je voudrais rester (deux) nuits.	I'd like to stay for (two) nights.	*zhe voo·drey res·tey (der) nwee.*
Du (deux juillet) au (six juillet).	From (July 2) to (July 6).	*dew (de zhwee·yey) o (see zhwee·yey).*
Est-ce que je peux la voir ?	Can I see it?	*es·ke zhe peu la vwar ?*
Est-ce que je peux camper ici ?	Am I allowed to camp here?	*es·ke zhe peu kom·pey ee·see ?*
Où est le terrain de camping le plus proche ?	Where's the nearest camp site?	*oo ey luh tey·run de kom·peeng le plew prosh ?*
Quand/Où le petit déjeuner est-il servi ?	When/Where is breakfast served?	*kon/oo le pe·tee dey·zhe·ney ey·teel sair·vee ?*
Réveillez-moi à (sept) heures, s'il vous plaît !	Please wake me at (seven)!	*rey·vey·yey·mwa a (set) eur seel voo pley !*
Est-ce que je pourrais avoir la clé, s'il vous plait ?	Could I have my key, please?	*es·ke zhe poo·rey a·vwar la kley seel voo pley ?*
Est-ce que je peux avoir une autre (couverture) ?	Can I get another (blanket)?	*es·ke zhe pe a·vwar ewn o·tre (koo·vair·tewr) ?*

Listen to Track 116

Avez-vous un ...	Is there a/an ...	a·vey·voo un ...
... ascenseur ?	... elevator?	... a·son·seur ?
... coffre-fort ?	... safe?	... ko·fre·for ?
C'est trop ...	The room is too ...	sey tro ...
... cher.	... expensive.	... shair.
... bruyant.	... noisy.	... brew·yon.
... petit.	... small.	... pe·tee.
... ne fonc-tionne pas.	... doesn't work.	... ne fong·syon pa.
La climatisation...	The air conditioning ...	la klee-ma-tee-za-syoñ ...
Le ventilateur ...	The fan ...	luh von-tee-la-tewr ...

Listen to Track 117

Les toilettes ...	The toilet ...	lay twa·let ...
... n'est pas propre (ne sont pas propres).	... isn't clean (aren't clean).	... ney pa pro·pre (nuh son pa pro.pre).
Quand faut-il régler?	What time is checkout?	kon fo·teel rey·gley
Puis-je laisser mes bagages ?	Can I leave my luggage here?	pweezh ley·sey mey ba·gazh
Est-ce que je pourrais avoir ..., s'il vous plait ?	Could I have my..., please?	es·ke zhe poo·rey a·vwar ... seel voo pley ?
... ma caution,	... deposit,	... ma ko·syon,
... mon passeport,	... passport,	... mon pas·por,
... mes biens précieux,	... valuables,	... mey byun prey·syeu,

Chapter 6.2: Weather and season / La météo et les saisons

Listen to Track 118

Quel temps fait-il ?	What's the weather like?	_kel tahn fey·teel ?_
Le temps est couvert.	It's cloudy.	_le tahn ey koo·vair._
Il fait froid.	It's cold.	_eel fey frwa._
Il fait chaud.	It's hot.	_eel fey sho._
Il pleut.	It's raining.	_eel pleu._
Il neige.	It's snowing.	_eel nezh._
Il fait beau.	It's sunny.	_eel fey bo._
Il fait chaud.	It's warm.	_eel fey sho._
Il y a du vent.	It's windy.	_eel ya dew von._
printemps m	spring	_prun·tahn_
été m	summer	_ey·tey_
automne m	autumn	_o·ton_
hiver m	winter	_ee·vair_

Chapter 6.3: Disabled travelers / Les voyageurs en situation de handicap

Listen to Track 119

Qu'est-ce que vous avez comme aménagements pour les handicapés ?	What facilities do you have for disabled people?	_kes kuh voo za-vay kom a-may-nazh-mahñ poor lay zahñ-dee-ka-pay ?_
Est-ce qu'il y a des toilettes pour handicapés ?	Are there any toilets for the disabled?	_es keel ya day twa-let poor ahñ-dee-ka-pay ?_
Avez-vous des chambres au rez-de chaussée ?	Do you have any bedrooms on the ground floor?	_a-vay voo day shahñbr oh ray duh shohsay ?_
Est-ce qu'il y a un ascenseur ?	Is there a lift?	_es keel ya uñ na-sahñ-sur ?_
Où est l'ascenseur ?	Where is the lift?	_oo eh la-sahñ-sur ?_
Est-ce qu'il y a des fauteuils roulants ?	Do you have wheelchairs?	_es keel ya day foh-tuh-yuh roo-lahñ ?_
On peut visiter ... en fauteuil roulant ?	Can you visit ... in a wheelchair?	_oñ puh vee-zee-tay ahñ foh-tuh-yuh roolahñ ?_
Est-ce que vous avez une boucle pour mal-entendants ?	Do you have an induction loop?	_es kuh voo za-vay ewñ bookl poor mal-ahñ- tahñ-dahñ ?_

Est-ce qu'il y a une réduction pour les handicapés ?	Is there a discount for disabled people?	*es keel ya ewn ray-dewk-syoñ poor layzahñ-dee-ka-pay ?*
Est-ce qu'il y a un endroit où on peut s'asseoir ?	Is there somewhere I can sit down?	*es keel ya uñ nahñ-drwa oo oñ puh sa-swar ?*

Chapter 6.4: Traveling with kids / Voyager avec des enfants

Listen to Track 120

Un billet tarif enfant.	A child's ticket.	*un bee-yeh ta-reef ahñ-fahñ.*
Il/Elle a ... ans.	He/She is ... years old.	*eel/el a ahñ.*
Est-ce qu'il y a une réduction pour les enfants ?	Is there a discount for children?	*es keel ya ewn ray-dewk-syoñ poor lay zahñ-fahñ ?*
Est-ce que vous avez un menu enfant ?	Do you have a children's menu?	*es kuh voo za-vay uñ muh-new ahñ- fahñ ?*
On peut y aller avec des enfants ?	Is it okay to take children?	*on puh ee a-lay a-vek day zahñ-fahñ ?*
Avez-vous ...	Do you have ...	*a-vay voo ...*
... une chaise de bébé / une chaise haute ?	... a high chair?	*... ewn shez duh bay-bay / ewn shez ot ?*
... un lit d'enfant ?	... a cot?	*... uñ lee dahñ-fahñ ?*
J'ai deux enfants.	I have two children.	*zhay duh zahñ-fahñ.*
Il/Elle a dix ans.	He/She is 10 years old.	*eel/el a dee zahñ.*
Est-ce que vous avez des enfants ?	Do you have any children?	*es kuh voo za-vay day zahñ-fahñ ?*

Chapter 7: Money, banking, and shopping / L'argent et les achats

Whether you like saving money or blowing it before it even reaches your wallet, financial matters are a core part of everyday life. Having the ability to talk about money and a good understanding of monetary terms in French will be highly useful when using your French in real-life scenarios. If you are traveling in a French-speaking country, you will at some point need to ask how much something costs or have other such questions related to financial expenses.

Chapter 7.1: Money / L'argent

Listen to Track 121

distributeur	cash dispenser	*dees-tree-bew-tur*
retrait espèces	cash withdrawal	*ruh-treh es-pes*
Où est-ce que je peux changer de l'argent ?	Where can I change some money?	*oo es kuh zhuh puh shahñ-zhay duh larzhahñ ?*
La banque ouvre quand ?	When does the bank open?	*la bahñk oovr kahñ ?*
La banque ferme quand ?	When does the bank close?	*la bahñk fehrm kahñ ?*
Je peux payer en livres sterling/ en euros ?	Can I pay with pounds/euros?	*zhuh puh pay-yay ahñ leevr stehr-leeng/ahñ nuh-roh ?*
Je peux utiliser ma carte (de crédit) dans ce distributeur ?	Can I use my credit card with this cash dispenser?	*zhuh puh ew-tee-lee-zay ma kart (duh kraydee) dahñ suh dee-stree-bew-tur ?*
Vous avez de la monnaie ?	Do you have any change?	*voo za-vay duh la mo-neh ?*

Chapter 7.2: Banking / La banque

Listen to Track 122

Où est la banque la plus proche ?	Where is the nearest bank?	*oo eh la bahnk la plew prawsh ?*
À quel guichet puis-je encaisser ceci ?	At which window can I cash this?	*ah kel ghee-sheh PWEE-zhuh tooshay suhsee ?*
Pouvez-vous me changer ceci ?	Can you change this for me?	*poo-vay-voo muh shahn-zhay suhsee ?*
Voulez-vous encaisser un chèque ?	Will you cash a check?	*voo-lay-voo pay-yay uhn shek ?*
Ne me donnez pas de gros billets.	Do not give me large bills.	*nuh muh daw-nay pah duh groh bee-yeh.*
Puis-je avoir de la petite monnaie ?	May I have some change?	*pwee-zha-vwahr uh la puh-teet maw-neh ?*
Une lettre de crédit.	A letter of credit.	*ewn LEH-truh duh kray-dee.*
Une lettre de change.	A bank draft.	*ewn LEH-truh duh shahnzh.*
Quel est le cours du change ?	What is the exchange rate?	*keh leh luh koor dew shahnzh ?*
Où est ...	Where's ...	*oo ey ...*
... le guichet automatique ?	... the ATM?	*... le gee·shey o·to·ma·teek ?*
... le bureau de change ?	... the foreign exchange office?	*... le bew·ro de shonzh ?*

Listen to Track 123

Je voudrais ...	I'd like to ...	*zhe voo·drey*
... faire un virement.	... arrange a transfer.	*... fair un veer·mon.*
... encaisser un chèque.	... cash a check.	*... ong·key·sey un shek.*
... changer de l'argent.	... change money.	*... shon·zhey de lar·zhon.*
... une avance de crédit.	... get a cash advance.	*... ewn a·vons de krey·dee.*
... retirer de l'argent.	... withdraw money.	*... re·tee·rey de lar·zhon.*
Quel est ...	What's ...	*kel ey ...*
... le tarif ?	... the charge for that?	*... le ta·reef ?*
... le taux de change ?	... the exchange rate?	*... le to de shonzh ?*
C'est ...	It's ...	*sey ...*
... (douze) euros.	... (12) euros.	*... (dooz) eu·ro.*
... gratuit.	... free.	*... gra·twee.*
À quelle heure ouvre la banque ?	What time does the bank open?	*a kel eur oo·vre la bongk ?*
Mon argent est-il arrivé ?	Has my money arrived yet?	*mon ar·zhon ey·teel a·ree·vey ?*

Chapter 7.3: Paying / Payer

Listen to Track 124

l'addition	the bill (restaurant)	_la-dee-syoñ bill_
la note	the bill (hotel)	_la not_
la facture	the invoice	_la fak-tewr_
la caisse	the desk	_la kes cash_
C'est combien? / Ça fait combien ?	How much is it?	_say koñ-byañ/sa feh koñ-byañ ?_
Ça fera combien ?	How much will it be?	_sa fuh-ra koñ-byañ ?_
Je peux payer...	Can I pay...	_zhuh puh pay-yay..._
... par carte de crédit ?	... by credit card?	_... par kart duh kray-dee ?_
... par chèque ?	... by check?	_... par shek ?_

Listen to Track 125

Mettez-le sur ma note !	Put it on my bill! (hotel)!	_meh-tay luh sewr ma not !_
L'addition, s'il vous plaît.	The bill, please. (restaurant)	_la-dee-syoñ seel voo pleh._
Où doit-on payer ?	Where do I pay?	_oo dwa-toñ pay-yay ?_
Vous acceptez les cartes de credit ?	Do you take credit cards?	_voo zak-sep-tay lay kart duh kray-dee ?_
Le service est compris ?	Is service included?	_luh sehr-vees ay koñ-pree ?_

Pourriez-vous me donner un reçu, s'il vous plait ?	Could you give me a receipt, please?	*poo-ree-ay voo muh do-nay uñ ruh-sew, seel voo pleh ?*
Est-ce qu'il faut payer à l'avance ?	Do I pay in advance?	*es keel foh pay-yay a la-vahñs ?*
Je suis désolé(e) ...	I'm sorry ...	*zhuh swee day-zo-lay ...*
... Je n'ai pas de monnaie.	... I don't have anything smaller / I don't have change.	*... zhuh nay pa duh mo-neh.*

Chapter 7.4: Luggage / Les bagages

Listen to Track 126

le retrait de bagages	baggage claim	*luh ruh-treh duh ba-gazh*
la consigne	left luggage	*la koñ-see-nyuh*
le chariot à bagages	luggage trolley	*luh sha-ryoh a ba-gazh*
Mes bagages ne sont pas encore arrivés.	My luggage hasn't arrived yet.	*may ba-gazh nuh soñ pa ahñ-kor a-reevay.*
Ma valise a été abîmée pendant le vol.	My suitcase has been damaged on the flight.	*ma va-leez a ay-tay a-bee-may pahñ- dahñ luh vol.*

Chapter 7.5: Repairs / Les réparations

Listen to Track 127

le cordonnier	shoe repairer	*luh kor-don-yay*
Réparations minute.	Repairs while you wait.	*ray-pa-ra-syoñ mee-newt.*
C'est cassé.	This is broken.	*say ka-say.*
Où est-ce que je peux le faire réparer ?	Where can I get this repaired?	*oo es kuh zhuh puh luh fehr ray-pa-ray ?*
Pouvez-vous réparer ...	Can you repair ...	*poo-vay voo ray-pa-ray ...*
... ces chaussures ?	... these shoes?	*... say shoh-sewr ?*
... ma montre ?	... my watch?	*... ma moñtr ?*

Chapter 7.6: Shopping

Listen to Track 128

Je veux faire les magasins.	I want to go shopping.	*zhuh vuh koo-reer lay ma-ga-zen.*
J'aime cela.	I like that.	*zhem suh-la.*
Combien est-ce ?	How much is it?	*kawn-byen ess ?*
C'est très cher.	It is very expensive.	*seh treh shehr.*
Je préfère quelque chose de mieux (de moins cher).	I prefer something better (cheaper).	*zhuh pray-fehr kel-kuh-shawz duh myuh (duh mwen shehr).*
Montrez-m'en d'autres.	Show me some others.	*mawn-tray-mahn DOH-truh.*
Puis-je l'essayer ?	May I try this on?	*PWEE-zhuh lehsay-yay ?*
Puis-je en commander un ?	Can I order one?	*pwee-zhahn kaw-mahn-day uhn ?*
Combien de temps cela prendra-t-il ?	How long will it take?	*kawn-byen duh tahn suh-la-prahn-dra-teel ?*
Veuillez prendre mes mesures.	Please take my measurements.	*vuh-yay PRAHN-druh may muh-zewr.*
Pouvez-vous l'expédier à New-York ?	Can you ship it to New York City?	*poo-vay-voo lex-pay-dyay ah New York ?*
À qui dois-je payer ?	Whom do I pay?	*ah kee DWAH-zhuh peh-yay ?*

Listen to Track 129

Veuillez m'envoyer la facture.	Please bill me.	*vuh-yay mahn-vwah-yay lafak-tewr.*
Je veux acheter un bonnet de bain.	I want to buy a bathing cap.	*zhuh vuh zash-tay uhn baw-neh duh ben.*
un maillot de bain	a bathing suit	*uhn kawss-tewm duh ben*
un soutien-gorge	a brassiere	*uhn soo-tyen-gawrzh*
une robe	a dress	*ewn rawb*
une blouse	a blouse	*ewn blooz*
un manteau	a coat	*uhn mahn-toh*
une paire de gants	a pair of gloves	*ewn pehr duh gahn*
un sac à main	a handbag	*uhn sak ah men*
des mouchoirs	some handkerchiefs	*day mooshwahr*
un chapeau	a hat	*uhn sha-poh*
une veste	a jacket	*ewn vaist*
de la lingerie	some lingerie	*duh la lenzh-ree*
une chemise de nuit	a nightgown	*ewn shuh-meez duh nwee*

Listen to Track 130

un imperméable	a raincoat	*uh nen-peh-may-ah-bluh*
une paire de chaussures	a pair of shoes	*ewn pehr duh shohsewr*
des lacets	some shoelaces	*day la-seh*

une paire de pantoufles	a pair of slippers	*ewn pehr duh pahn-too-fluh*
une paire de chaussettes	a pair of socks	*ewn pehr duh shohset*
une paire de bas nylon	a pair nylon	*ewn pehr duh bah nee-lawn*
un costume	a suit	*uhn kawss-tewm*
un pull	a sweater	*uhn sweh-tuhr*
des cravates	some ties	*day krah-vaht*
un pantalon	trousers	*uhn pahn-ta-lawn*
des sous-vêtements	some underwear	*day soo-vet-mahn*

Listen to Track 131

Avez-vous des cendriers ?	Do you have some ashtrays?	*a-vay-voo day sahn-dree-ay ?*
une boîte de bonbons	a box of candy	*ewn bwaht duh bawn-bawn*
de la porcelaine	some porcelain (china)	*duh la pawrsuh-len*
des poupées	some dolls	*day poo-pay*
des boucles d'oreille	some earings	*day boo-kluh daw-ray*
du parfum	some perfume	*dew par-fuhn*
des tableaux	some pictures	*day ta-bloh*
des disques	some records	*day deesk*
de l'argenterie	some silverware	*duh lar-zhahn-tree*
des jouets	some toys	*day zhoo-eh*
un parapluie	an umbrella	*uhn pa-ra-plwee*
une montre	a watch	*ewn mawn-truh*

Listen to Track 132

Où est	Where's ...	oo ay ...
... la banque ?	... the bank?	... la bongk ?
... la librairie ?	... the bookshop?	... la lee·brey·ree ?
... le magasin photo ?	... the camera shop?	... le ma·ga·zun fo·to ?
... le grand magasin ?	... the department store?	... le gron ma·ga·zun ?
... l'épicerie ?	... the grocery store?	... ey·pee·sree ?
... le marchand de journaux ?	... the newsagency?	... le mar·shon de zhoor·no ?
... le supermarché ?	... the supermarket?	... le sew·pair·mar·shey ?
Où puis-je acheter (un cadenas)?	Where can I buy (a padlock)?	oo pweezh ash·tey (un kad·na) ?
Je cherche ...	I'm looking for ...	zhe shairsh ...
Est-ce que je peux le voir ?	Can I look at it?	es·ke zhe peu le vwar ?
Vous en avez d'autres ?	Do you have any others?	voo zon a·vey do·tre ?
Est-ce qu'il y a une garantie ?	Does it have a guarantee?	es keel ya ewn ga·ron·tee ?
Pouvez-vous me l'envoyer à l'étranger ?	Can I have it sent overseas?	poo·vey·voo me lon·vwa·yey a ley·tron·zhey ?

Puis-je faire réparer mon/ ma/mes ?	Can I have my ... repaired?	*pwee·zhe fair rey·pa·rey mon/ ma/may ?*
C'est défectueux.	It's faulty.	*sey dey·fek·tweu.*

Listen to Track 133

Je voudrais ..., s'il vous plaît.	I'd like ..., please.	*zhe voo·drey seel voo pley.*
... un sac,	... a bag,	*... un sak,*
... un remboursement,	... a refund,	*... un rom· boors·mon,*
... rapporter ceci,	... to return this,	*... ra·por·tey se·see,*
Pouvez-vous écrire le prix ?	Can you write down the price?	*poo·vey·voo ey·kreer le pree ?*
C'est trop cher.	That's too expensive.	*sey tro shair.*
Vous pouvez baisser le prix ?	Can you lower the price?	*voo poo·vey bey·sey le pree ?*
Je vous donnerai (cinq) euros.	I'll give you (five) euros.	*zhe voo don·rey (sungk) eu·ro.*
Il y a une erreur dans la note.	There's a mistake in the bill.	*eel ya ewn ey·reur don la not.*
Est-ce que je peux payer avec ...	Do you accept ...	*es·ke zhe pe pey·yey a·vek*
... une carte de crédit ?	... credit cards?	*... ewn kart de krey·dee ?*
... une carte de débit ?	... debit cards?	*... ewn kart de dey·bee ?*
Ma monnaie ?	My change?	*ma mo·ney ?*
un reçu	a receipt	*un re·sew*

Chapter 7.7: Laundry / Faire la lessive

Listen to Track 134

le pressing	dry-cleaner's	*luh preh-seeng*
la laverie automatique	launderette/ laundromat	*la lav-ree oh-to-ma-teek*
la lessive en poudre	washing powder / laundry detergent	*la leh-seev ahñ poodr*

Chapter 7.8: To Complain / Se plaindre

Listen to Track 135

Ça ne marche pas.	This doesn't work.	*Sa nuh marsh pa.*
C'est sale.	It's dirty.	*Say sal.*
Le/La ... ne marche pas.	The ... doesn't work.	*Luh/la ... nuh marsh pa.*
Les ... ne marchent pas.	The ... don't work.	*Lay ... nuh marsh pa.*
... la lumière	... the light	*... la lew-myehr*
... la serrure	... the lock	*... la seh-rewr*
... le chauffage	... the heating	*... luh shoh-fazh*
... la climatisation	... the air conditioning	*.... la klee-ma-tee-za-syoñ*
C'est cassé.	It's broken.	*say ka-say.*
Je veux être remboursé (e).	I want a refund.	*zhuh vuh etr rahñ-boor-say.*

Chapter 7.9: Problems / Les problèmes

Listen to Track 136

Pouvez-vous m'aider ?	Can you help me?	*poo-vay voo meh-day ?*
Je parle très peu français.	I speak very little French.	*zhuh parl treh puh Ihñ-seh.*
Est-ce qu'il y a quelqu'un qui parle anglais ici ?	Does anyone here speak English?	*es keel ya kel-kuñ kee parl ahñ-gleh ee-see ?*
Je voudrais parler au responsable.	I would like to speak to whoever is in charge.	*zhuh voo-dreh par-lay oh reh-spoñ-sabl*
Je me suis perdu(e).	I'm lost.	*zhuh muh swee pehr-dew.*
pour aller à/au ... ?	How do I get to ...?	*poor a-lay a/ oh ... ?*
J'ai raté ...	I missed ...	*zhay ra-tay ...*
... mon train.	... my train.	*... moñ trañ.*
... mon avion.	... my plane.	*... moñ na-vyoñ.*
.. ma correspondance.	... my connection.	*... ma ko-res-poñ-dahñs.*
J'ai raté mon avion à cause d'une grève.	I've missed My flight because there was a strike.	*zhay ra-tay moñ na-vyoñ a kohz dewn grev.*
Le car est parti sans moi.	The coach has left without me.	*luh kar ay par-tee sahñ mwa.*

Pouvez-vous me montrer comment ça marche ?	Can you show me how this works?	*poo-vay voo muh moñ-tray ko-mahñ sa marsh ?*
J'ai perdu mon porte-monnaie.	I have lost my purse.	*zhay pehr-dew moñ port-mo-neh.*
Je dois aller à/au (etc.) ...	I need to get to ...	*zhuh dwa a-lay a/oh ...*
Laissez-moi tranquil(le) !	Leave me alone!	*leh-say mwa trahñ-keel !*
Allez-vous en !	Go away!	*a-lay voo zahñ !*

Chapter 7.10: Emergencies / Les urgences

Listen to Track 137

S'il vous plaît, appelez ...	Please call ...	*seel voo pleh, a-puh-lay ...*
... la police.	... the police.	*... la po-lees.*
... une ambulance.	... an ambulance.	*... ewn ahñ-bew-lahñs.*
... les pompiers.	... the fire brigade.	*... poñ-pyay*
... le commissariat.	... the police station (in large towns).	*... ko-mee-sar-ya*
... la gendarmerie.	... the police station (in villages and small towns).	*... zhahñ-darm-ree*
... les urgences.	... the accident and emergency department.	*... ewr-zhahñs*
Au secours !	Help!	*oh skoor !*
Au feu !	Fire!	*oh fuh !*
Pouvez-vous m'aider ?	Can you help me?	*poo-vay voo meh-day ?*
Il y a eu un accident.	There has been an accident.	*eel ya ew uñ nak-see-dahñ.*
Il y a un blessé.	Someone has been injured.	*eel ya uñ bleh-say.*
Il/elle a été renversé(e) par une voiture.	He/she has been knocked down by a car.	*eel/el a ay-tay rahñ-vehr-say par ewn vwa-tewr.*

Listen to Track 138

Où est le commissariat ?	Where is the police station?	*oo eh luh ko-mee-sar-ya ?*
Je veux signaler un vol.	I want to report a theft.	*zhuh vuh seen-ya-lay uñ vol.*
On m'a volé/ attaqué(e).	I've been robbed/ attacked.	*oñ ma vo-lay/a-ta-kay.*
On m'a violée.	I've been raped.	*oñ ma vee-o-lay.*
Je veux parler à une femme agent de police.	I want to speak to a policewoman.	*zhuh vuh par-lay a ewn fam a-zhahñ duh po-lees.*
On m'a vole ...	Someone has stolen ...	*oñ ma vo-lay ...*
... mon sac à main.	... my handbag.	*... moñ sak a mañ.*
... mon argent.	... my money.	*... moñ nar-zhahñ.*
On a forcé ma voiture.	My car has been broken into.	*oñ na for-say ma vwa-tewr.*
On m'a volé ma voiture.	My car has been stolen.	*oñ ma vo-lay ma vwa-tewr.*
Il faut que je passe un coup de téléphone.	I need to make a telephone call.	*eel foh kuh zhuh pas uñ koo duhtay-lay-fon.*
Il me faut un constat pour mon assurance.	I need a report for my insurance.	*eel muh foh uñ kon-sta poor moñ na-sew-rahñs.*

More emergency phrases related to road, car, and traffic:

__Listen to Track 139__

Je ne savais pas quelle était la limite de vitesse.	I didn't know the speed limit.	*zhuh nuh sa-veh pa kel ay-teh la lee-meet duh vee-tes.*
C'est une amende de combien ?	How much is the fine?	*say tewn a-mahñd duh koñ-byañ ?*
Où dois-je la payer ?	Where do I pay it?	*oo dwa-zhuh la pay-yay ?*
Est-ce qu'il faut la payer immédiatement ?	Do I have to pay it straight away?	*es keel foh la pay-yay ee-may-dyat-mahñ ?*
Je suis vraiment désolé(e), monsieur l'agent.	I'm very sorry, officer.	*zhuh swee vray-mahñ day-zo-lay, muh-syuh la-zhahñ.*
Vous avez brûlé un feu rouge.	You went through a red light.	*voo za-vay brew-lay uñ fuh roozh.*
Vous n'avez pas cédé la priorité.	You didn't give way.	*voo na-vay pa say-day la pree-o-ree-tay.*

Chapter 8: Health and wellness / Santé et bien-être

If you are traveling to a French-speaking country, you will need to know some health-related vocabulary. Whether you require pain-killers from the pharmacy or have an emergency doctor's visit while abroad, you will likely encounter health-related situations and it is an invaluable skill to be able to speak the necessary French to navigate such issues.

Chapter 8.1: At the pharmacy / La pharmacie

Listen to Track 140

La pharmacie	Pharmacy / Chemist's	*la far-ma-see*
Une pharmacie (de nuit)	A (night) pharmacist	*ewn far·ma·see (de nwee)*
La pharmacie de garde	Duty chemist's.	*la far-ma-see duh gard.*
Avez-vous quelque chose pour ...	Can you give me something for ...	*a-vay voo kel-kuh shohz poor ...*
... le mal de tête ?	... a headache?	*... luh mal duh tet ?*
... le mal des transports ?	... car sickness?	*... luh mal day trahñ-spor ?*
... la grippe ?	... flu?	*... la greep ?*
... la diarrhée ?	... diarrhea?	*... la dya-ray ?*
... les coups de soleil ?	... sunburn?	*... lay koo duh so-leh-yuh ?*

C'est sans danger pour les enfants ?	Is it safe for children?	*say sahñ dahñ-zhay poor lay zahñ-fahñ ?*
Combien je dois lui en donner ?	How much should I give him/her?	*koñ-byañ zhuh dwa lwee ahñ do-nay ?*

Chapter 8.2: Dealing with medical issues and seeing a doctor / Faire face à des problèmes médicaux et consulter un médecin

Listen to Track 141

un médecin	a doctor	un meyd·sun
un hôpital	a hospital	u·no·pee·tal
J'ai besoin d'un médecin(qui parle anglais).	I need a doctor (who speaks English).	zhey be·zwun dun meyd·sun (kee parl ong·gley).
Est-ce que je peux voir une femme médecin ?	Could I see a female doctor?	es·ke zhe peu vwar ewn fam meyd·sun ?
Je n'ai plus de médicaments.	I've run out of my medication.	zhe ney plew de mey·dee·ka·mon.
Je suis malade.	I'm sick.	zhe swee ma·lad.
J'ai une douleur ici.	It hurts here.	zhey ewn doo·leur ee·see.

Listen to Track 142

J'ai ...	I have (a) ...	zhey ...
... de l'asthme.	... asthma.	... de las·me.
... une bronchite.	... bronchitis.	... bron·sheet
... de la constipation.	... constipation.	... la kon·stee·pa·syon.
... de la toux.	... cough.	... la too
... de la diarrhée.	... diarrhea.	... la dya·rey

... de la fièvre.	... fever.	*... la fyev·re*
... mal à la tête.	... headache.	*... mal a la tet.*
... une maladie de cœur.	... heart condition.	*... ma·la·dee de keur*
... la nausée.	... nausea.	*... la no·zey.*
... une douleur.	... pain.	*... ewn doo·leur.*
... mal à la gorge.	... sore throat.	*... mal a la gorzh.*
... mal aux dents.	... toothache.	*... mal o don.*

Listen to Track 143

Je suis aller- gique ...	I am allergic ...	*zhe swee za-lair- zheek ...*
... aux antibiotiques.	... to antibiotics.	*... o zon· tee·byo·teek.*
... aux antiin- flammatoires.	... to anti- inflammatories.	*... o zun·tee·un· fla·ma·twar.*
... à l'aspirine.	... to aspirin.	*... a las·pee·reen.*
... aux piqûres d'abeilles.	... to bee stings.	*... o za·bey·ye*
... à la codéine.	... to codeine.	*... a la ko·dey·een.*
... à la pénicilline.	... to penicillin.	*... a la pey·nee· see·leen.*
antiseptique.	antiseptic.	*on·tee·sep·teek.*

pansement m	bandage	*pons·mon*
préservatifs m pl	condoms	*prey·zair·va·teef*
contraceptifs m pl	contraceptives	*kon·tra·sep·teef*
médicament pour la diarrhée	diarrhea medicine	*may-dee-ka-mon poor la dya-rey*

Listen to Track 144

répulsif anti-insectes m	insect repellent	*rey·pewl·seef on·tee·un·sekt*
laxatifs m pl	laxatives	*lak·sa·teef*
analgésiques m pl	painkillers	*a·nal·zhey·zeek*
sels de réhydratation m pl	rehydration salts	*seyl de rey·ee·dra·ta·syon*
somnifères m pl	sleeping tablets	*som·nee·fair*
Je désire voir un médecin américain.	I wish to see an American doctor.	*zhuh day-zeer vwahr uhn a-may-ree-ken.*
Je ne dors pas bien.	I do not sleep well.	*zhuh nuh dawr pah byen.*
J'ai mal à la tête.	I have a headache.	*zhay mal ah la tet.*
Dois-je rester au lit ?	Must I stay in bed?	*dwah-zhuh res-tay oh lee ?*
Puis-je me lever ?	May I get up?	*pwee-zhuh muh luh-vay ?*
Je me sens mieux.	I feel better.	*zhuh muh sahn myuh.*

urgences	accident and emergency department	*ewr-zhahñs*

Listen to Track 145

consultations	consultations	*koñ-sewl-ta-syoñ*
Je me sens mal.	I feel ill.	*zhuh muh sahñ mal.*
Vous avez de la fièvre ?	Do you have a temperature?	*voo za-vay duh la fyehvr ?*
Non, J'ai mal ici.	No, I have a pain here.	*noñ, zhay mal ee-see.*
Mon fils/Ma fille est malade.	My son/My daughter is ill.	*moñ fees/ma fee ay ma-lad.*
Je suis diabétique.	I'm diabetic.	*zhuh swee dya-bay-teek.*
Je suis enceinte.	I'm pregnant.	*zhuh swee ahñ-sañt.*
Je prends la pilule.	I'm on the pill.	*zhuh prahñ la pee-lewl.*
Je suis allergique à la pénicilline.	I'm allergic to penicillin.	*zhuh swee za-lehr-zheek a la pay-nee-seeleen.*
Faut-il la/le transporter à l'hôpital ?	Will she/he have to go to the hospital?	*foh-teel la/luh trahñ-spor-tay a lo-pee-tal ?*
Est-ce que je dois payer ?	Will I have to pay?	*es kuh zhuh dwa pay-yay ?*
Combien ça va coûter ?	How much will it cost?	*koñ-byañ sa va koo-tay ?*
Il me faut un reçu pour l'assurance.	I need a receipt for the insurance.	*eel muh foh uñ ruh-sew poor la-sew-rahñs.*

Chapter 8.3: At the dentist / Chez le dentiste

Listen to Track 146

J'ai besoin de voir un dentiste.	I need to see a dentist.	*zhay buh-zwañ duh vwar uñ dahñ-teest.*
Il/Elle a mal aux dents.	He/She has toothache.	*eel/el a mal oh dahñ.*
Pouvez-vous me faire un plombage proviso ire ?	Can you do a temporary filling?	*poo-vay voo muh fehr uñ ploñ-bazh ?*
Pouvez-vous me donner quelque chose contre la douleur ?	Can you give me something for the pain?	*poo-vay voo muh do-nay kel-kuh shohz koñtr la doo-lur ?*
Ça me fait mal.	It hurts.	*sa muh feh mal.*
Pouvez-vous me réparer mon dentier ?	Can you repair my dentures?	*poo-vay voo muh ray-pa-ray moñ dahñtyay ?*
Je dois payer ?	Do I have to pay?	*zhuh dwa pay-yay ?*
Combien ça va coûter ?	How much will it be?	*koñ-byañ sa va koo-tay ?*
Il me faut un reçu pour mon assurance.	I need a receipt for my insurance.	*eel muh foh uñ ruh-sew poor moñ na-sewrahñs.*

Chapter 9: Miscellaneous / Thèmes divers

If you want more additional phrases 😊

Chapter 9.1: Liquid / Les liquides (mesures de capacité)

Listen to Track 147

un demi-litre de ...	1/2 litre of ...	*uñ duh-mee leetr duh ...*
un litre de ...	a litre of ...	*uñ leetr duh ...*
une demi-bouteille de ...	1/2 bottle of ...	*ewn duh-mee-boo-tay-yuh duh ...*
une bouteille de ...	a bottle of ...	*ewn boo-tay-yuh duh ...*
un verre de ...	a glass of ...	*uñ vehr duh ...*

Chapter 9.2: Quantity / Quantités

Listen to Track 148

cent grammes de ...	100 grams of ...	*sahñ gram duh ...*
un demi-kilo de ...	a half kilo of ...	*uñ duh-mee kee-loh duh ...*
un kilo de ...	a kilo of ...	*uñ kee-loh duh ...*
une tranche de ...	a slice of ...	*ewn trahñsh duh ...*
une portion de ...	a portion of ...	*ewn por-syoñ de ...*
une douzaine de ...	a dozen ...	*ewn doo-zen duh ...*
une boîte de ...	a box of ...	*ewn bwat duh ...*
un paquet de ...	a packet of ...	*uñ pa-keh duh ...*
une brique de ...	a carton of ...	*ewn breek duh ...*
un pot de ...	a jar of ...	*uñ poh duh ...*
pour 500 euros de ...	500 euros of ...	*Poor sañk-son uh-roh duh...*
un quart	a quarter	*uñ kar*
dix pour cent	ten per cent	*dee poor sahñ*
plus de	more	*plews duh*
moins de	less	*mwañ duh*
assez de ...	enough of ...	*a-say duh ...*
le double	double	*luh doobl*
deux fois	twice	*duh fwa*

Chapter 9.3: Cardinal numbers / les nombres cardinaux

Listen to Track 149

zéro	0	*zay-roh*
un	1	*uñ*
deux	2	*duh*
trois	3	*trwa*
quatre	4	*katr*
cinq	5	*sañk*
six	6	*sees*
sept	7	*set*
huit	8	*weet*
neuf	9	*nuhf*
dix	10	*dees*
onze	11	*oñz*
douze	12	*dooz*
treize	13	*trez*
quatorze	14	*ka-torz*
quinze	15	*kañz*
seize	16	*sez*
dix-sept	17	*dees-set*
dix-huit	18	*deez-weet*
dix-neuf	19	*deez-nuhf*
vingt	20	*vañ*
vingt et un	21	*vañ tay uñ*
vingt-deux	22	*vañt-duh*
vingt-trois	23	*vañt-trwa*

Listen to Track 150

trente	30	*trahñt*
quarante	40	*ka-rahñt*
cinquante	50	*sañk-ahñt*
soixante	60	*swa-sahñt*
soixante-dix	70	*swa-sahñt-dees*
soixante et onze	71	*swa-sahñt-ay-oñz*
soixante-douze	72	*swa-sahñt-dooz*
quatre-vingts	80	*katr-vañ*
quatre-vingt-un	81	*katr-vañ-un*
quatre-vingt-deux	82	*katr-vañ-duh*
quatre-vingt-dix	90	*katr-vañ-dees*
quatre-vingt-onze	91	*katr-vañ-oñz*
cent	100	*sahñ*
cent dix	110	*sahñ dees*
deux cents	200	*duh sahñ*
deux cent cinquante	250	*duh sahñ sañk-ahñt*
mille	1,000	*meel*
un million	one million	*uñ mee-lyoñ*

Chapter 9.4: Asking and telling time/ Demander et dire l'heure

Listen to Track 151

Il est quelle heure?/Quelle heure est-il ?	What time is it?	*eel ay kel ur?/kel ur ay-teel ?*
Il est ...	It's...	*eel ay ...*
... deux heures.	... two o'clock.	*... duh zur.*
... trois heures.	... three o'clock.	*... trwa zur.*
... six heures.	... six o'clock.	*... see zur.*
Il est une heure.	It's one o'clock.	*eel ay (t) ewn ur.*
Il est minuit.	It's midnight.	*eel ay mee-nwee.*
Il est neuf heures.	It is nine.	*nuh vur*
Il est neuf heures dix.	It is ten past nine.	*nuh vur dees*
Il est neuf heures quinze.	It is a quarter past nine.	*nuh vur*
Il est neuf heures et demie/neuf heures trente.	It is 9:30. / It is half past nine.	*nuh vur ay duh-mee/nuh vur trahñt*
Il est dix heures moins vingt-cinq.	It is 25 to ten. / It is 9:35.	*dee zur mwañ vañt-sañk*

Listen to Track 152

Il est dix heures moins le quart.	It is a quarter to 10.	*dee zur mwañ luh kar.*
Il est dix heures moins dix.	It is 10 to 10.	*dee zur mwañ dees*
Il à quelle heure ...	When does it ...	*eel ... a kel ur ...*
... ouvre/ ferme/ commence/ finit ?	... open/close/ begin/finish?	*... oovr/fehrm/ ko-mahñs/fee-nee ?*
à trois heures	at three o'clock	*a trwa zur*
avant trois heures	before three o'clock	*a-vahñ trwa zur*
après trois heures	after three o'clock	*a-preh trwa zur*
aujourd'hui	today	*oh-zhoor-dwee*
ce soir	tonight	*suh swar*
demain	tomorrow	*duh-mañ*
hier	yesterday	*ee-yehr*

Chapter 9.5: Days of the week / Les jours de la semaine

Listen to Track 153

lundi	Monday	*luñ-dee*
mardi	Tuesday	*mar-dee*
mercredi	Wednesday	*mehr-kruh-dee*
jeudi	Thurday	*zhuh-dee*
vendredi	Friday	*vahñ-druh-dee*
samedi	Saturday	*sam-dee*
dimanche	Sunday	*dee-mahñsh*
hier	yesterday	*ee-yehr*
demain	tomorrow	*duh-mañ*
aujourd'hui	today	*oh-zhoor-dwee*
ce soir	tonight	*suh swar*
avant-hier	the day before yesterday	*ahvang tee yehr*
la veille	last night	*lah vay-yuh*
après-demain	the day after tomorrow	*ahpray duh-mañ*
le matin	the morning	*luh mahtañ*
l'après-midi	the afternoon	*lah pray meedee*
le soir	the evening	*luh swar*
la nuit	the night	*lah nwee*
la semaine prochaine	next week	*lah suh main proshañ*
la semaine dernière	last week	*lah suh main dehrnyair*

Chapter 9.6: Months of the year/ Les mois de l'année

Listen to Track 154

janvier	January	*zhahñ-vyay*
février	February	*fay-vree-yay*
mars	March	*mars*
avril	April	*av-reel*
mai	May	*meh*
juin	June	*zhwañ*
juillet	July	*zhwee-yeh*
août	August	*oo(t)*
septembre	September	*sep-tahñbr*
octobre	October	*ok-tobr*
novembre	November	*no-vahñbr*
décembre	December	*day-sahñbr*

Chapter 9.7: Colors / Les couleurs

Listen to Track 155

vert	green	_vair_
bleu	blue	_bluh_
rouge	red	_rooj_
noir	black	_nwahr_
rose	pink	_rohz_
blanc	white	_blahn_
orange	orange	_Aw-rahnzh_
jaune	yellow	_zhohn_
gris	grey	_gree_
violet	purple	_vyaw-leh_
brun	brown	_bruhn_

Chapter 9.8: Measurements/ Les mesures

Listen to Track 156

Quelle est la longueur ?	What is the length?	*keh leh la lawn-guhr ?*
... la largeur ?	... the width?	*... la lar-zhuhr ?*
... la pointure ?	... the size?	*... la pwen-tewr ?*
Combien le mètre ?	How much is it per meter?	*kawn-byen luh MEH-truh ?*
Il a dix mètres de long sur quatre mètres de large.	It is ten meters long by four meters wide.	*eel a dee MEH-truh duh lawn sewr KA-truh MEH-truh duh larzh.*
haut	high	*oh*
bas	low	*bah*
grand	large	*grahn*
petit	small	*puh-tee*
moyen	medium	*mwah-yen*
semblable	alike	*sâhn-bla-bluh*
différent	different	*dee-fay-rahn*
une paire	a pair	*ewn pehr*
une douzaine	a dozen	*ewn doo-zen*
une demi-douzaine	a half dozen	*ewn duh-mee-doo-zen*

Conclusion

Before I end this book and say goodbye, I would like to thank you and add a few more things.

1. I'd love to hear from you!

Would it be too much to ask what you think about this book? If you can spare a few minutes, please let me know your thoughts by contacting me at contact@talkinfrench.com. I would be delighted to receive any feedback from you.

Perhaps you can also share your honest opinion on ways I could further improve this book. I am always looking forward to suggestions on how I could be of more help to French language learners like you.

2. I hope you will enjoy (or already enjoyed) your travel to France.

If you have more questions about French travel and culture, please feel free to use the available resources in the "Talk in French" website. You'll find plenty of updated articles there about all things French: food, music, movies, TV shows, novels, and many more. Just head over to the culture section (https://www.talkinfrench.com/category/french-culture/).

3. If you are learning to speak French (or planning to), please consider my other products.

I have plenty of available materials on learning French – grammar, vocabulary, a study guide for all levels, French short stories, podcasts, and complete step-by-step methods. You can check them all out at the Talk in French Store (https://store.talkinfrench.com/).

And so with that, we say our goodbyes.

A bientôt !

Frédéric Bibard

How to download the audio?

Please take note that the audio files are in MP3 format and need to be accessed online. No worries though; it's quite easy!

On your computer, smartphone, iPhone/iPad or tablet, simply go to this link:

https://www.talkinfrench.com/phrasebook-audio/

Did you have any problems downloading the audio? If you did, feel free to send an email to support@talkinfrench. com. We'll do our best to assist you, but we would greatly appreciate it if you could thoroughly review the instructions first.

Merci,

Frederic

About the author

Frédéric Bibard is the founder of TalkinFrench.com, a French language and culture website, consistently named by bab.la and Lexiophiles as the top French language learning blog for 2014, 2015, and 2016.

Frédéric spent several years teaching French while traveling abroad. He has since returned to Paris to dedicate his time to developing fun and helpful French language resources.

He takes food seriously (he is French, after all), but he complements it with a love for running, which allows him to nurture his passion for good food while staying in shape.

Say hello to him on Twitter (@fredericbibard) and Google+, or visit his website: www.talkinfrench.com

French Crash Course: A Seven-Day Guide to Learning Basic French (with Audio!)

- **An innovative approach to learning French:** Speed up language learning by focusing on French lessons you need to get by in a French-speaking environment.

- **Learn Basic French in a week:** Get seven days of high-impact French language lessons with structured daily lessons, exercises, and culture immersion activities.

- **FREE audio material:** Learn how to speak and pronounce French properly and improve your listening comprehension skills.

Learn More:

https://www.amazon.com/dp/107824572X

A Complete Audio Method for French Language Learning

LEARN FRENCH
FOR BEGINNERS

A Complete Audio Method
For French Language Learning

By Talk In French

Narrated by

- Batouly Sylla
- Emmanuelle Solo
- François Noble

- Four weeks of easy-to-follow daily audio lessons
- Practical dialogues based on real-life scenarios
- 900+ most frequently-used French vocabulary
- Speaking practice, quizzes, and review lessons

Learn More:

https://geni.us/beginnerfrench